Professional English in Use

Finance

Ian MacKenzie

CAMBRIDGE
UNIVERSITY PRESS

CAMBRIDGE UNIVERSITY PRESS
Cambridge, New York, Melbourne, Madrid, Cape Town, Singapore, São Paulo

Cambridge University Press
The Edinburgh Building, Cambridge CB2 2RU, UK

www.cambridge.org
Information on this title: www.cambridge.org/9780521616270

First published 2006

Printed in Italy by Printer Trento

A catalogue record for this publication is available from the British Library

ISBN-13 978-0-521-61627-0 Student's Book
ISBN-10 0-521-61627-1 Student's Book

Produced by Kamae Design

Contents

BANKING

CORPORATE FINANCE

Introduction

Who is this book for?

Professional English in Use Finance is designed to help intermediate and upper-intermediate learners of business English improve their financial vocabulary – and perhaps their knowledge of finance. It is for people studying English before they start work as well as for those already working who need English in their job.

You can use the book on your own for self-study, or with a teacher in the classroom, one-to-one, or in groups.

How is the book organized?

The book has 50 two-page thematic units, in four areas of finance: **accounting, banking, corporate finance**, and **economics and trade**.

The left-hand page of each unit explains new words and expressions, and the right-hand page allows you to check and develop your understanding of them and how they are used, through a series of exercises.

There is **cross-referencing** between units to show connections between the same word or similar words used in different contexts.

There is also a **Language reference** section, giving examples of idioms used to describe changes in the price of financial assets; showing how to say and write numbers and how to stress English words; and listing differences between British and American financial vocabulary.

There is an **answer key** at the back of the book. Most of the exercises have questions with only one correct answer. But some of the exercises, including the **Over to you** activities at the end of each section (see opposite), are designed for writing and/or discussion about yourself and your own organization, or one you would like to work for.

There is also an **index**. This lists all the new words and expressions introduced in the book, and gives the unit numbers in which they appear. The index also tells you how the words and expressions are pronounced.

The left-hand page

This page introduces new vocabulary for each thematic area. The presentation is divided into sections indicated by letters – usually A, B and C – with simple, clear titles.

As well as explanations of vocabulary, there is information about typical word combinations and the grammar associated with particular vocabulary, for example the verbs that are typically used with certain nouns.

There are also notes on language points, including differences between British and American English.

The right-hand page

The exercises on the right-hand page give practice in using the new vocabulary presented on the left-hand page. Sometimes the exercises concentrate on using the words and expressions presented on the left-hand page in context. Other exercises test your understanding of the concepts on the left-hand page. Some units contain diagrams or tables to complete, or crosswords.

'Over to you' sections

An important feature of *Professional English in Use Finance* is the **Over to you** section at the end of each unit. The **Over to you** sections give you the chance to put into practice the words and expressions in the unit in relation to your own professional situation, studies or opinions. For some of them you will need to find information on the internet or in newspapers.

Self-study learners can do this section as a written activity.

In the classroom, the **Over to you** sections can be used as the basis for discussion with the whole class, or in small groups with a spokesperson for each group summarizing the discussion and its outcome for the class. The teacher can then get learners to look again at the exercises relating to points that have caused difficulty. Learners can follow up by using the **Over to you** section as a written activity, for example as homework.

How to use the book for self-study

Find the topic you are looking for by referring to the contents page or the index. Read through the explanations on the left-hand page of the unit. Do the exercises on the right-hand page. Check your answers in the key. If you have made some mistakes, go back and look at the explanations and exercise again. Note down important words and expressions in your notebook.

How to use the book in the classroom

Teachers can choose units that relate to learners' particular needs and interests, for example areas they have covered in course books, or that have come up in other activities. Alternatively, lessons can contain a regular vocabulary slot, where learners look systematically at the vocabulary of particular thematic areas.

Learners can work on the units in pairs, with the teacher going round the class assisting and advising. Teachers should get learners to think about the logical process of the exercises, pointing out why one answer is possible and others are not.

Cambridge International Certificate in Financial English (ICFE)

Professional English in Use Finance is an ideal self-study or classroom companion for students who are preparing for the Cambridge International Certificate in Financial English (ICFE). Cambridge ICFE is set at levels B2 and C1 of the Council of Europe's Common European Framework of Reference for Languages (CEF). The exam is designed to determine whether candidates whose first language is not English have an adequate level of English to function efficiently, in terms of language ability, within the international finance community.

Cambridge ICFE is for finance students and those already employed in or seeking employment in any finance setting. It is also intended to help employers in international finance with the hiring and training of personnel, and to assist finance faculties and course providers with selection, placement and graduation of students.

We hope you enjoy using this book.

1 Money and income

A Currency

The money used in a country – euros, dollars, yen, etc. – is its **currency**. Money in **notes** (**banknotes**) and **coins** is called **cash**. Most money, however, consists of **bank deposits:** money that people and organizations have in bank accounts. Most of this is **on paper** – existing in theory only – and only about ten per cent of it exists in the form of cash in the bank.

BrE: note or banknote; AmE: bill

B Personal finance

All the money a person receives or **earns** as payment is his or her **income**. This can include:

- a **salary:** money paid monthly by an employer, or **wages**: money paid by the day or the hour, usually received weekly
- **overtime:** money received for working extra hours
- **commission:** money paid to salespeople and agents – a certain percentage of the income the employee generates
- a **bonus:** extra money given for meeting a target or for good financial results
- **fees:** money paid to professional people such as lawyers and architects
- **social security:** money paid by the government to unemployed and sick people
- a **pension:** money paid by a company or the government to a retired person.

Salaries and wages are often paid after deductions such as social security charges and pension contributions.

Amounts of money that people have to **spend** regularly are **outgoings**. These often include:

- **living expenses:** money spent on everyday needs such as food, clothes and public transport
- **bills:** requests for the payment of money owed for services such as electricity, gas and telephone connections
- **rent:** the money paid for the use of a house or flat
- a **mortgage:** repayments of money borrowed to buy a house or flat
- **health insurance:** financial protection against medical expenses for sickness or accidental injuries
- **tax:** money paid to finance government spending.

A financial plan, showing how much money a person or organization expects to earn and spend is called a **budget**.

BrE: social security; AmE: welfare
BrE: flat; AmE: apartment

Planned monthly budget for next year (€)			
Income		**Outgoings**	
Salary (after deductions)	3,250	Rent	900
Commission (average)	600	Bills	250
		Living expenses	1,200
		Health insurance	130
		Tax	800
Total	**3,850**	Total	**3,280**

1.1 Complete the sentences with words from the box. Look at A and B opposite to help you.

commission	bonus	currency	earn	mortgage	tax
overtime	pension	rent	salary	social security	

1 After I lost my job, I was living on .... for three months. This was difficult, because the amount was much lower than the .... I had before.

2 I used to work as a salesperson, but I wasn't very successful, so I didn't .... much ....

3 If the company makes 10% more than last year, we'll all get a .... at the end of the year.

4 It'll take me at least 25 years to repay the .... on my house.

5 Many European countries now have the same ...., the euro.

6 My wages aren't very good, so I do a lot of ....

7 Nearly 40% of everything I earn goes to the government as ....

8 The owner has just increased the .... on our flat by 15%.

9 When I retire, my .... will be 60% of my final salary.

1.2 Are the following statements true or false? Find reasons for your answers in A and B opposite.

1 Bank deposits are not classified as money.
2 People earning wages get paid more often than people earning a salary.
3 People working on commission always get paid the same amount.
4 When you stop working at the end of your career, you receive a pension.
5 Most people pay a rent and a mortgage.

Over to you

Do you know what the average income is in your country, and in your job, or the one you are studying for? How important is salary in your choice of career?

2 Business finance

A Capital

When people want to **set up** or start a company, they need money, called **capital**. Companies can **borrow** this money, called a **loan**, from banks. The loan must be paid back with **interest**: the amount paid to borrow the money. Capital can also come from issuing **shares** or **equities** – certificates representing units of ownership of a company. (See Unit 29) The people who **invest** money in shares are called **shareholders** and they **own** part of the company. The money they provide is known as **share capital**. Individuals and financial institutions, called **investors**, can also **lend** money to companies by buying **bonds** – loans that pay interest and are repaid at a fixed future date. (See Unit 33)

Money that is **owed** – that will have to be paid – to other people or businesses is a **debt**. In accounting, companies' debts are usually called **liabilities**. Long-term liabilities include bonds; short-term liabilities include debts to suppliers who provide goods or services **on credit** – that will be paid for later.

The money that a business uses for everyday expenses or has available for spending is called **working capital** or **funds**.

BrE: shares; AmE: stocks
BrE: shareholder; AmE: stockholder

B Revenue

All the money coming into a company during a given period is **revenue**. Revenue minus the cost of sales and operating **expenses**, such as rent and salaries, is known as **profit**, **earnings** or **net income**. The part of its profit that a company pays to its shareholders is a **dividend**. Companies pay a proportion of their profits to the government as **tax**, to finance government spending. They also **retain**, or keep, some of their earnings for future use.

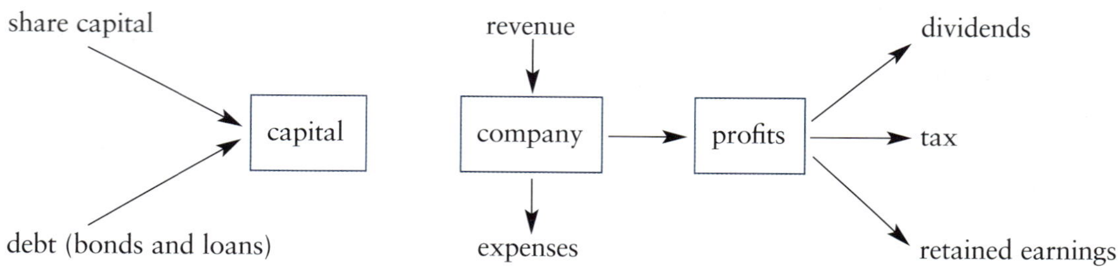

C Financial statements

Companies give information about their financial situation in **financial statements**. The **balance sheet** shows the company's **assets** – the things it owns; its liabilities – the money it owes; and its capital. The **profit and loss account** shows the company's revenues and expenses during a particular period, such as three months or a year.

BrE: profit and loss account; AmE: income statement

2.1 Complete the crossword. Look at A, B and C opposite to help you.

Across

3 Small companies often try to get bank loans when they need to .... money. (6)
5 We don't have sufficient .... to build a completely new factory. (5)
7 and 6 down Details of a company's liabilities are shown on the .... (7,5)
8 We're going to raise more money by selling new shares to our existing .... (12)
12 We had to raise €50,000 .... in order to start the business. (7)
13 We're going to pay back some of the people who lent us money, and reduce our .... (4)
14 I decided to buy a $10,000 .... instead of shares, as it's probably safer. (4)
16 Another term for profit is net .... (6)
18 I think this is a good investment: it pays 8% .... (8)
20 When they saw our financial statements, the bank refused to .... us any more money. (4)
21 Profit is the difference between revenue and .... (8)

Down

1 The profit and .... account shows if a company is receiving more money than it's spending. (4)
2 If you don't like taking risks, you should only .... in very successful companies. (6)
4 A company's retained earnings belong to its .... (6)
6 See 7 across.
9 Anything a company uses to produce goods or services is an .... (5)
10 The company made such a big profit, I expected a higher .... (8)
11 We sold a lot more last year, so our .... went up. (7)
15 We .... our suppliers $100,000 for goods bought on credit. (3)
17 Everyone who buys a share .... part of the company. (4)
19 Thirty per cent of our profits goes straight to the government in .... (3)

"It's been a great year – let's hope we can keep the shareholders from finding out."

Over to you

Think of the company you work for, or one that you are interested in. How was it financed when it was set up, and how is it financed now?

3 Accounting and accountancy

A Accounting

- **Accounting** involves **recording** and summarizing an organization's **transactions** or business deals, such as purchases and sales, and reporting them in the form of financial statements. (See Units 11–14) In many countries, the accounting or **accountancy** profession has professional organizations which operate their own training and examination systems, and make technical and ethical rules: these relate to accepted ways of doing things.
- **Bookkeeping** is the day-to-day recording of transactions.
- **Financial accounting** includes bookkeeping, and **preparing** financial statements for shareholders and **creditors** (people or organizations who have lent money to a company).
- **Management accounting** involves the use of accounting data by managers, for making plans and decisions.

B Auditing

Auditing means examining a company's systems of control and the **accuracy** or exactness of its records, looking for errors or possible **fraud**: where the company may have deliberately given false information.

- An **internal audit** is carried out by a company's own **accountants** or **internal auditors**.
- An **external audit** is done by **independent auditors**: auditors who are not employees of the company.

The external audit examines the truth and fairness of financial statements. It tries to prevent what is called '**creative accounting**', which means recording transactions and values in a way that produces a false result – usually an artificially high profit.

There is always more than one way of presenting accounts. The accounts of British companies have to give a **true and fair view** of their financial situation. This means that the financial statements must give a correct and reasonable picture of the company's current condition.

C Laws, rules and standards

In most continental European countries, and in Japan, there are **laws** relating to accounting, established by the government. In the US, companies whose stocks are traded on public stock exchanges have to **follow rules** set by the Securities and Exchange Commission (SEC), a government agency. In Britain, the rules, which are called **standards**, have been established by independent organizations such as the Accounting Standards Board (ASB), and by the accountancy profession itself. Companies are expected to **apply** or use these standards in their **annual accounts** in order to give a true and fair view.

Companies in most English-speaking countries are largely funded by shareholders, both individuals and financial institutions. In these countries, the financial statements are prepared for shareholders. However, in many continental European countries businesses are largely funded by banks, so accounting and financial statements are prepared for creditors and the tax authorities.

3.1 What type of work does each person do, and what is the name of each job? Look at A and B opposite to help you.

1 I record all the purchases and sales made by this department.

2 This month, I'm examining the accounts of a large manufacturing company.

3 I analyse the sales figures from the different departments and make decisions about our future activities.

4 I am responsible for preparing our annual balance sheet.

5 When the accounts are complete, I check them before they are presented to the external auditors.

3.2 Match the two parts of the sentences. Look at C opposite to help you.

1 In Britain
2 In most of continental Europe and Japan
3 In the USA
4 In Britain and the USA
5 In much of continental Europe

a accounting rules are established by a government agency.
b companies are mainly funded by shareholders or stockholders.
c accounting rules are set by an independent organization.
d the major source of corporate finance is banks.
e accounting rules are set by the government.

3.3 Find verbs in A, B and C opposite that can be used to make word combinations with the nouns below.

.... / .... **an audit**

.... / .... / .... **standards**

.... / .... / .... / .... **rules**

.... / .... **transactions**

Over to you

Is accounting in your country based on standards, rules, laws, or a mixture of these? What accounting system do international companies in your country use?

4 Bookkeeping

A Double-entry bookkeeping

Zaheer Younis works in the accounting department of a trading company:

'I began my career as a bookkeeper. **Bookkeepers** record the company's daily **transactions**: sales, purchases, debts, expenses, and so on. Each type of transaction is recorded in a separate **account** – the cash account, the liabilities account, and so on. **Double-entry bookkeeping** is a system that records two aspects of every transaction. Every transaction is both a **debit** – a deduction – in one account and a corresponding **credit** – an addition – in another. For example, if a company buys some **raw materials** – the substances and components used to make products – that it will pay for a month later, it debits its purchases account and credits the supplier's account. If the company sells an item on credit, it credits the sales account, and debits the customer's account. As this means the level of the company's **stock** – goods ready for sale – is reduced, it debits the stock account. There is a corresponding increase in its **debtors** – customers who owe money for goods or services purchased – and the debtors or accounts payable account is credited. Each account records debits on the left and credits on the right. If the bookkeepers do their work correctly, the total debits always equal the total credits.'

BrE: debtors; AmE: accounts receivable
BrE: creditors; AmE: accounts payable
BrE: stock; AmE: inventory

B Day books and ledgers

'For accounts with a large number of transactions, like purchases and sales, companies often record the transactions in **day books** or **journals**, and then put a daily or weekly summary in the main double-entry records.

In Britain, they call the main books of account **nominal ledgers**. **Creditors** – suppliers to whom the company owes money for purchases made on credit – are recorded in a **bought ledger**. They still use these names, even though these days all the information is on a computer.'

Note: In Britain the terms **debtors** and **creditors** can refer to people or companies that owe or are owed money, or to the sums of money in an account or balance sheet.

C Balancing the books

'At the end of an **accounting period**, for example a year, bookkeepers prepare a **trial balance** which transfers the debit and credit balances of different accounts onto one page. As always, the total debits should equal the total credits. The accountants can then use these balances to prepare the organization's financial statements.'

4.1 Match the words in the box with the definitions below. Look at A and B opposite to help you.

credit	ledger	debit
creditors	stock	debtors

1 an amount entered on the left-hand side of an account, recording money paid out
2 a book of accounts
3 customers who owe money for goods or services not yet paid for
4 an amount entered on the right-hand side of an account, recording a payment received
5 goods stored ready for sale
6 suppliers who are owed money for purchases not yet paid for

4.2 Complete the sentences. Look at A, B and C opposite to help you.

1 .... shows where money comes from and where it goes: it is always transferred from one .... to another one. Every event is entered twice – once as a credit and once as a ....
2 Most businesses record very frequent or numerous transactions in .... or ....
3 The main account books are called .... , and the book relating to creditors is called the ....
4 In order to prepare financial statements, companies do a .... which copies all the debit and credit balances of different accounts onto a single page.

4.3 Complete the sentences using 'debit' or 'credit'. Look at A opposite to help you.

1 If you buy new assets, you .... the cash or capital account.
2 If you pay some bills, you .... the liabilities account.
3 If you buy materials from a supplier on 60 days' credit, you .... the purchases account and .... the supplier's account.
4 If you sell something to a customer who will pay 30 days later, you .... the sales account and .... the customer's account.

Over to you

What qualities does a good bookkeeper need? Would you like to work as a bookkeeper? If not, which type of accounting do you think is the most interesting, and why?

5 Company law 1

A Partnerships

A **partnership** is a business arrangement in which several people work together, and share the risks and profits. In Britain and the US, partnerships do *not* have limited liability for debts, so the **partners** are fully liable or responsible for any debts the business has. Furthermore, partnerships are not legal entities, so in case of a legal action, it is the individual partners and not the partnership that is taken to court. In most continental European countries there are various kinds of partnership which *are* legal entities.

A **sole trader** business – an enterprise owned and operated by a single person – also has unlimited liability for debts.

B Limited liability

A **company** is a business that is a **legal entity**. In other words, it has a separate legal existence from its owners, the shareholders. It can enter into contracts, and can be sued or taken to court if it breaks a contract. A company can (in theory) continue for ever, even if all the staff and owners change. Most companies have **limited liability**, which means that the owners are not fully **liable for** – or responsible for – the business's debts. These companies are known as **limited companies**. Their liability is limited to the value of their **share capital**: the amount of cash that the shareholders have contributed to the company. This limitation of liability encourages investors to risk their money to become part owners of companies, while leaving the management of these companies to qualified managers and senior managers, known as **directors**.

These managers and full-time **executive directors** run the company for its owners. There are standard procedures of **corporate governance** – the way a company is run by the management for the shareholders, and how the managers are accountable to the shareholders. These include separating the job of **chairman** from that of **managing director**, and having several **non-executive directors** on the **board of directors** who do not work full-time for the company but can offer it expert advice. Non-executive directors are often more **objective**: less influenced by their opinions and beliefs. There is also an **audit committee**, containing several non-executive directors, to which the auditors report.

BrE: chairman; AmE: president
BrE: managing director; AmE: chief executive officer (CEO)

C Founding companies

When people **found** or start companies, they **draw up** or prepare **Articles of Association** and a **Memorandum of Association**. The Articles of Association state:

- the rights and duties of the shareholders and directors
- the relationships among different classes of shareholder (See Unit 29)
- the relationships between shareholders and the company and its directors.

The Memorandum of Association states:

- the company's name
- the location of the company's **registered office** – where to send official documents
- the company's **purpose** – its aims or objectives
- the **authorized share capital** – the maximum share capital it can have.

BrE: Articles of Association; AmE: Bylaws
BrE: Memorandum of Association; AmE: Certificate of Incorporation

5.1 Are the following statements true or false? Find reasons for your answers in A and B opposite.

1 In case of a legal dispute, people can take a company's shareholders to court.
2 The owners of limited companies have to pay all the company's debts.
3 Many companies are not owned by their managers.
4 External directors can usually give more objective advice than full-time directors.
5 Partners in British and American businesses are not liable for the partnership's debts.
6 In case of a dispute, people can take British companies and partnerships to court.

5.2 Make word combinations using a word from each box. Then match the word combinations to the definitions below. Look at A opposite to help you.

corporate	committee
audit	directors
limited	governance
non-executive	capital
share	liability

1 ....: a group of directors to whom the external auditors present their report
2 ....: members of a board of directors who are not full-time managers of the company
3 ....: owners' money invested in a company
4 ....: responsibility for debts up to the value of the company's share capital
5 ....: the way a company is managed for its owners

5.3 Complete the document. Look at C opposite to help you.

(a) ________________ of Association

1. The name of the Company is Language Services Pty Limited.
2. The (b) ________________ of the Company will be in Australia.
3. The (c) ________________ for which the Company is established is to provide translation and interpreting services to international companies.
4. The (d) ______________________ of the company is made up of ordinary shares divided into five thousand (5,000) shares of A$1.00 par value each with one vote for each share.

Over to you

Do partnerships have limited liability in your country? If not, who would you trust enough to start a partnership with?

6 Company law 2

A Private and public companies

Private companies usually have 'Limited' or 'Ltd' at the end of their name. They are not allowed to sell their stocks or shares on an open market. Most companies are private; there are about one million private companies in Britain, compared to around 2,000 **public limited companies** (**PLCs**). These companies have 'plc' at the end of their name, and their shares are publicly traded on the London Stock Exchange. A **stock exchange** is a market where anyone can buy stocks and shares. The US equivalent of a PLC is a company or **corporation** registered with the Securities and Exchange Commission (SEC).

SEC-registered companies, also known as **listed companies**, have to make **quarterly reports** (i.e. every three months). They report on:

- sales revenue or **turnover** – the money received by the company in that period from selling goods or services
- **gross profit** – turnover less cost of sales
- **net profit** – gross profit less administrative expenses and tax.

Companies on the London Stock Exchange, known as **quoted companies**, have to produce a half-yearly **interim report** which informs shareholders about the company's progress. These reports are not audited.

All companies with shareholders or stockholders have to send them an **Annual Report** each financial year. This contains a review of the year's activity, and an examination and explanation of the company's financial position and results. There are also financial statements and notes (see Units 11–14), and the **auditors' report** on the financial statements.

BARCLAYS PLC Interim Report 2004

- Group performance was very strong:
  – profit before tax up 23% to £2,411m
  – earnings per share up 25% at 26.7p
  – dividend per share up 17% to 8.25p
  – return on equity of 20.4%
- All businesses had higher profits, demonstrating good progress across the whole portfolio.
- Income growth was particularly strong, up 14%, with good broad based contributions by business and by income type.

B AGMs

Public companies have to hold an **Annual General Meeting** (**AGM**), and most private ones do too. At this meeting the shareholders can question directors about the content of the Annual Report and the financial statements, vote to accept or reject the dividend recommended by the directors, and vote on replacements for retiring members of the board. The meeting can also carry out any other business stated in the company's Memorandum of Association or Certificate of Incorporation, and Articles of Association or Bylaws.

If there is a crisis, the directors or the shareholders can request to hold an **Extraordinary General Meeting (EGM)** to discuss the situation. For example, if there are claims of **misconduct** by the directors, where they have behaved illegally, there could be an EGM.

BrE: Annual General Meeting (AGM); AmE: Annual Meeting of Stockholders
BrE: Extraordinary General Meeting (EGM); AmE: Special Meeting

6.1 Complete the table. Look at A and B opposite to help you.

<table>
<tr><th rowspan="2">(1) .... companies</th><th colspan="2">Public companies</th></tr>
<tr><td>in the UK</td><td>in the US</td></tr>
<tr><td rowspan="3">■ can't sell shares on the (2) ....</td><td>■ are called public (3) .... companies or (4) .... companies.</td><td>■ are called SEC-registered companies or (6) .... companies.</td></tr>
<tr><td>■ produce (5) .... reports.</td><td>■ produce (7) .... reports.</td></tr>
<tr><td colspan="2">■ publish an (8) .... and hold an (9) ....</td></tr>
</table>

6.2 Find words in A and B opposite with the following meanings.

1 behaviour that breaks the law
2 sales revenue minus the cost of sales, before deductions for administration expenses, interest charges, etc.
3 sales revenue minus the cost of making and selling the goods, and deductions for administration expenses, interest charges, etc.
4 the total amount of money a company receives from selling goods or services

6.3 Match the two parts of the sentences. Look at A and B opposite to help you.

1 Only quoted or listed companies
2 American corporations publish details
3 Companies' financial statements, and the auditor's report,
4 Quarterly and six-monthly reports
5 Shareholders can ask company directors questions
6 Companies can hold an emergency general meeting

a about their sales and profits every three months.
b are contained in their annual reports.
c are not checked by external auditors.
d if there is a crisis.
e can have their shares traded on a stock exchange.
f at an annual meeting.

Over to you

Have you ever been to an AGM? Was there any disagreement between the shareholders and the directors? Who do you think is usually more powerful – the shareholders or the directors?

7 Accounting policies and standards

A Valuation and measurement

Investors in companies want to know how much the companies are worth, so companies regularly have to publish the value of their assets and liabilities. Companies also have to calculate their profits or losses: their managers need this information, and so do shareholders, **bondholders** and the tax authorities.

Companies can choose their **accounting policies** – their way of doing their accounts. There are a range of methods of **valuation** – deciding how much something is worth – and **measurement** – determining how big something is – that are accepted by law or by official accounting standards. In the USA, there are Generally Accepted Accounting Principles (GAAP). In most of the rest of the world there are International Financial Reporting Standards (IFRS), set by the International Accounting Standards Board. These are technical rules or **conventions** – accepted ways of doing things that are not written down in a law.

Although businesses can choose among different accounting policies, they have to be consistent, which means using the same methods every year, unless there is a good reason to change a policy: this is known as the **consistency** principle. The policies also have to be **disclosed** or revealed to the shareholders: the Annual Report will contain a 'Statement of Accounting Policies' that mentions any changes that have been made. This enables shareholders to compare profits and values with those of previous years.

Areas in which the choice of policies can make a big difference to the final profit figure include **depreciation** – reducing the value of assets in the company's accounts (see Unit 9), the valuation of stock or inventory, and the making of **provisions** – amounts of money deducted from profits – for future pension payments.

As there is always more than one way of presenting accounts, the accounts of British companies have to give **a true and fair view** of their financial situation – meaning there are various possibilities – rather than *the* true and fair view – meaning only one is possible.

BrE: depreciation; AmE: depreciation, amortization
BrE: a true and fair view; AmE: a fair presentation

B Historical cost and inflation accounting

The aim of accounting standards (see Unit 3) is to provide shareholders with the information that will allow them to make financial decisions. This is one reason why in many countries accounting follows the **historical cost** principle: companies record the original purchase price of assets, and not their (estimated) current selling price or replacement cost. This is more objective, and the current value is not important if the business is a **going concern** – a successful company that will continue to do business – as its assets are not going to be sold, or do not currently need to be replaced.

However, some countries with regular high inflation, e.g. in South America, use **inflation accounting** systems that take account of changing prices. One system used is **replacement cost accounting**, which values all assets at their **current replacement cost** – the amount that would have to be paid to replace them now.

7.1 Match the two parts of the sentences. Look at A and B opposite to help you.

1 Companies' managers, investors, creditors and the tax authorities all
2 There are different ways of doing accounting but companies have to be consistent,
3 Companies have to disclose or make known
4 The historical cost principle is that the price paid to buy assets,
5 A going concern usually doesn't

a and not their current value, is recorded in accounts.
b need to know the current market value of its assets.
c need to know about the size of profits or losses.
d which accounting methods they are using.
e which means regularly using the same methods.

7.2 Are the following statements true or false? Find reasons for your answers in A and B opposite.

1 Companies are told which accounting policies to use.
2 Companies can change their accounting policies whenever they like, as long as they disclose this in their Annual Report.
3 Companies could produce several profit figures, depending on how they depreciated their assets, valued their inventory, etc.
4 There is only one correct interpretation of a company's financial position, and company accounts must show this.
5 In a lot of countries, companies do not record the current value of their assets.
6 In countries with high inflation, companies value their assets at their current replacement cost.

7.3 Complete the table with words from A and B opposite and related forms. Put a stress mark in front of the stressed syllable in each word. The first one has been done for you.

Verb	Noun(s)	Adjective
	calcu'lation	–
–		consistent
–		conventional
measure		–
present		–
		valuable

Over to you

Which are the most important accounting standards or rules in your country – GAAP, IFRS, IAS, or something else?

8 Accounting assumptions and principles

A Assumptions

When writing accounts and financial statements, accountants have to follow a number of assumptions, principles and conventions. An **assumption** is something that is generally accepted as being true. The following are the main assumptions used by accountants:

- The **separate entity** or **business entity** assumption is that a business is an accounting unit separate from its owners, creditors and managers, and their assets. These people can all change, but the business continues as before.
- The **time-period** assumption states that the economic life of the business can be divided into (artificial) time periods such as the **financial year**, or a quarter of it.
- The **continuity** or **going concern** assumption says that a business will continue into the future, so the current market value of its assets is not important. (See Unit 7)
- The **unit-of-measure** assumption is that all financial transactions are in a single monetary unit or currency. Companies with **subsidiaries** – that is, other companies that they own – in different countries have to convert their results into one currency in **consolidated financial statements** for the whole group of companies.

BrE: financial year;
AmE: fiscal year

B Principles

The following are the most important accounting principles (as well as the **consistency** principle and the **historical cost** principle, mentioned in Unit 7):

- The **full-disclosure** principle states that financial reporting must include *all* significant information: anything that makes a difference to the users of financial statements.
- The principle of **materiality**, however, says that very small and unimportant amounts do not need to be shown.
- The principle of **conservatism** is that where different accounting methods are possible, you choose the one that is least likely to overstate or over-estimate assets or income.
- The **objectivity** principle says that accounts should be based on facts and not on personal opinions or feelings. Accounts, therefore, should be **verifiable**: it should be possible for internal and external auditors to show that they are true. This isn't always possible, however: depreciation or amortization, and provisions for bad debts, for example, are necessarily **subjective** – based on opinions.
- The **revenue recognition** principle is that revenue is recognized in the accounting period in which it is earned. This means the revenue is recorded when a service is provided or goods delivered, not when they are paid for.
- The **matching** principle, which is related to revenue recognition, states that each cost or expense related to revenue earned must be recorded in the same accounting period as the revenue it helped to earn.

"New from accounting, sir. Two and two is four again"

8.1 Match the accounting assumptions and principles (1–6) to the activities they prevent (a–f). Look at A and B opposite to help you.

1 conservatism principle
2 matching principle
3 separate entity assumption
4 revenue recognition principle
5 time-period assumption
6 unit-of-measure assumption

a showing a profit divided into US dollars, euros, Swiss francs, etc.
b publishing financial statements for a 15-month period, because this will show better profits
c waiting until customers pay before recording revenue
d waiting until customers pay before recording expenses
e listing the owners' personal assets in a company's financial statements
f valuing assets and estimating future revenue at the highest possible figures

8.2 Complete the sentences. Look at A and B opposite to help you.

1 A company's .... does not have to begin on 1 January, like the calendar year.
2 If an American company owns a company in Britain, this is a ....
3 Multinationals, with companies in lots of different countries, combine all their results in one set of ....
4 Every entry in a company's accounts must be ....: there must be a document available showing that it is true.

8.3 Complete the table with words from A, B and C opposite and related forms. Put a stress mark in front of the stressed syllable in each word. The first one has been done for you. Then complete the sentences below with words from the table.

Verb	Noun	Adjective
as'sume		–
	disclosure	–
–	objectivity	
recognize		–
–	subjectivity	
	verification	

1 Both the internal and the external auditors have to .... the accounts.
2 Companies have to .... all relevant financial information in their annual reports.
3 Despite the .... principle, accountants have to make some subjective judgements.
4 Even if a company is going through a bad period, for accounting purposes we .... it's a going concern.

Over to you

Look at the Annual Reports of one or two companies. How many of the assumptions and principles described here are mentioned in the notes to the financial statements?

9 Depreciation and amortization

A Fixed assets

A company's assets are usually divided into **current assets** like cash and stock or inventory, which will be used or converted into cash in less than a year, and **fixed assets** such as buildings and equipment, which will continue to be used by the business for many years. But fixed assets **wear out** – become unusable, or become **obsolete** – out of date, and eventually have little or no value. Consequently fixed assets are **depreciated**: their value on a balance sheet is reduced each year by a **charge against profits** on the profit and loss account. In other words, part of the cost of the asset is deducted from the profits each year.

The accounting technique of **depreciation** makes it unnecessary to charge the whole cost of a fixed asset against profits in the year it is purchased. Instead it can be charged during all the years it is used. This is an example of the matching principle. (See Unit 8)

BrE: fixed assets; AmE: property, plant and equipment

B Valuation

Assets such as buildings, machinery and vehicles are grouped together under fixed assets. Land is usually not depreciated because it tends to **appreciate**, or gain in value. British companies occasionally **revalue** – calculate a new value for – appreciating fixed assets like land and buildings in their balance sheets. The revaluation is at either **current replacement cost** – how much it would cost to buy new ones, or at **net realizable value** (**NRV**) – how much they could be sold for. This is not allowed in the USA. Apart from this exception, **appreciation** is only recorded in countries that use inflation accounting systems. (See Unit 7)

Companies in countries which use historical cost accounting – recording only the original purchase price of assets – do not usually record an estimated **market value** – the price at which something could be sold today. The conservatism and objectivity principles support this; and where the company is a going concern, the market value of fixed assets is not important. (See Units 7 and 8)

C Depreciation systems

The most common system of depreciation for fixed assets is the **straight-line method**, which means charging equal annual amounts against profit during the lifetime of the asset (e.g. deducting 10% of the cost of an asset's value from profits every year for 10 years). Many continental European countries allow **accelerated depreciation**: businesses can deduct the whole cost of an asset in a short time. Accelerated depreciation allowances are an **incentive** to investment: a way to encourage it. For example, if a company deducts the entire cost of an asset in a single year, it reduces its profits, and therefore the amount of tax it has to pay. Consequently new assets, including huge buildings, can be valued at zero on balance sheets. In Britain, this would not be considered a true and fair view of the company's assets.

"Let's see, it says here that you've had a lot of corporate accounting experience ..."

9.1 Match the words in the box with the definitions below. Look at A and B opposite to help you.

appreciate	current assets	fixed assets
obsolete	revalue	wear out

1 to record something at a different price
2 assets that will no longer be in the company in 12 months' time
3 to increase rather than decrease in value
4 out of date, needing to be replaced by something newer
5 assets that will remain in the company for several years
6 to become used and damaged

9.2 Match the nouns in the box with the verbs below to make word combinations. Then use some of the word combinations to complete the sentences below. Look at A, B and C opposite to help you.

costs	fixed assets	market value
profits	value	purchase price

deduct ....

record ....
....

depreciate ....

reduce ....
....

1 Because we .... the .... , we don't have worry about the market value of fixed assets.
2 To depreciate .... , we .... part of their .... from profits each year.
3 Because land usually appreciates, companies do not generally .... its .... on the balance sheet.

9.3 Match the two parts of the sentences. Look at B and C opposite to help you.

1 All fixed assets can appreciate if there is high inflation,
2 Accelerated depreciation allows companies to
3 Fixed assets generally lose value, except for land,
4 The straight-line method of depreciation
5 Accelerated depreciation reduces companies' tax bills,

a which usually appreciates.
b charges equal amounts against profits every year.
c remove some extremely valuable assets from their balance sheets.
d which encourages them to invest in new factories, etc.
e but historical cost accounting ignores this.

Over to you

Are companies in your country allowed to record huge assets, such as their headquarters, as having zero value on their balance sheets? Is this a good idea?

10 Auditing

A Internal auditing

After bookkeepers complete their accounts, and accountants prepare their financial statements, these are checked by **internal auditors**. An **internal audit** is an **examination** of a company's accounts by its own internal auditors or **controllers**. They **evaluate** the **accuracy** or correctness of the accounts, and check for errors. They make sure that the accounts **comply with**, or follow, established policies, procedures, standards, laws and regulations. (See Units 7 and 8) The internal auditors also check the company's **systems of control**, related to recording transactions, valuing assets and so on. They check to see that these are adequate or sufficient and, if necessary, **recommend** changes to existing policies and procedures.

B External auditing

Public companies have to **submit** their financial statements to **external auditors** – independent auditors who do not work for the company. The auditors have to give an opinion about whether the financial statements represent a true and fair view of the company's financial situation and results. (See Unit 3)

During the audit, the external auditors examine the company's systems of internal control, to see whether transactions have been **recorded** correctly. They check whether the assets mentioned on the balance sheet actually exist, and whether their valuation is correct. For example, they usually check that some of the debtors recorded on the balance sheet are genuine. They also check the annual **stock take** – the count of all the goods held ready for sale. They always look for any unusual items in the company's **account books** or statements.

Until recently, the big auditing firms also offered **consulting** services to the companies whose accounts they audited, giving them advice about business planning, strategy and restructuring. But after a number of big financial scandals, most accounting firms separated their auditing and consulting divisions, because an auditor who is also getting paid to advise a client is no longer totally independent.

BrE: stock take;
AmE: count of the inventory

C Irregularities

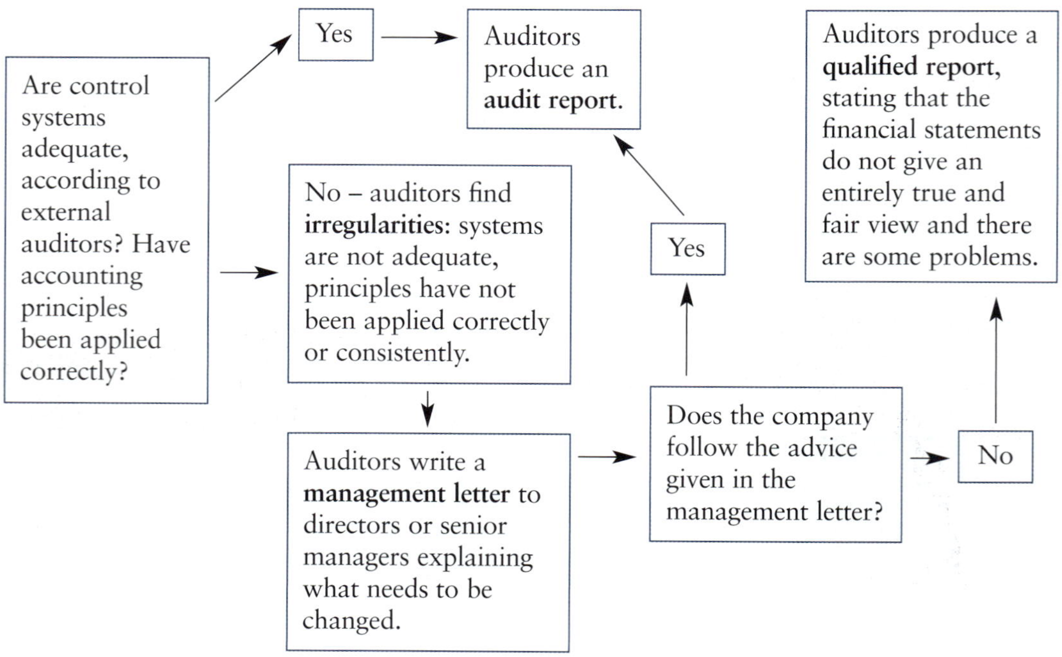

10.1

Match the job titles (1–4) with the descriptions (a–d). Look at A and B opposite to help you.

1 bookkeepers
2 accountants
3 internal auditors
4 external auditors

a company employees who check the financial statements
b expert accountants working for independent firms who review companies' financial statements and accounting records
c people who prepare financial statements
d people who prepare a company's day-to-day accounts

10.2

Match the nouns in the box with the verbs below to make word combinations. Some words can be used twice. Look at A and B opposite to help you.

accounts	procedures	opinions
systems of control	regulations	policies
stock take	advice	laws

check ....
....
....

examine ....
....

comply with ....
....
....
....

give ....
....

10.3

Complete the table with words from A, B and C opposite and related forms. Put a stress mark in front of the stressed syllable in each word. The first one has been done for you. Then complete the sentences below with the correct forms of words from the table.

Verb	Noun	Adjective
–		'accurate
	compliance	–
recommend		
	record	–
	examination	–

1 I'm an internal auditor. I .... the company's accounts, to make sure that they are .... , and that they .... with company policies and general accounting principles.
2 If the control systems aren't adequate, I make .... concerning changes.
3 The external auditors check to see if transactions are being .... correctly.

Over to you

Would you like to work as an external auditor? Do you think they get a very friendly welcome at the companies whose accounts they audit? If not, why not?

11 The balance sheet 1

A Assets, liabilities and capital

Balance Sheet, 31 December 20_ _ ($'000)

Current assets	3,500	Liabilities	6,000
Fixed assets	6,500	Shareholders' equity	4,000
Total assets	10,000	Total liabilities and Shareholders' equity	10,000

Company law in Britain, and the Securities and Exchange Commission in the US, require companies to publish annual **balance sheets:** statements for shareholders and creditors. The balance sheet is a document which has two halves. The totals of both halves are always the same, so they balance. One half shows a business's **assets,** which are things owned by the company, such as factories and machines, that will bring future economic benefits. The other half shows the company's **liabilities,** and its **capital** or **shareholders' equity** (see below). Liabilities are obligations to pay other organizations or people: money that the company **owes,** or will owe at a future date. These often include loans, taxes that will soon have to be paid, future pension payments to employees, and bills from **suppliers:** companies which provide raw materials or parts. If the suppliers have given the buyer a period of time before they have to pay for the goods, this is known as **granting credit.** Since assets are shown as debits (as the cash or capital account was debited to purchase them), and the total must correspond with the total sum of the credits – that is the liabilities and capital – **assets equal liabilities plus capital** (or **A = L + C**).

American and continental European companies usually put assets on the left and capital and liabilities on the right. In Britain, this was traditionally the other way round, but now most British companies use a vertical format, with assets at the top, and liabilities and capital below.

BrE: balance sheet; AmE: balance sheet or statement of financial position
BrE: shareholders' equity; AmE: stockholders' equity

B Shareholders' equity

Shareholders' equity consists of all the money belonging to shareholders. Part of this is **share capital** – the money the company raised by selling its shares. But shareholders' equity also includes **retained earnings:** profits from previous years that have not been **distributed** – paid out to shareholders – as dividends. Shareholders' equity is the same as the company's net assets, or assets minus liabilities.

A balance sheet does not show how much money a company has spent or received during a year. This information is given in other financial statements: the **profit and loss account** and the **cash flow statement.** (See Unit 14)

11.1 Are the following statements true or false? Find reasons for your answers in A and B opposite.

1 British and American balance sheets show the same information, but arranged differently.
2 The revenue of the company in the past year is shown on the balance sheet.
3 The two sides or halves of a balance sheet always have the same total.
4 The balance sheet gives information on how much money the company has received from sales of shares.
5 The assets total is always the same as the liabilities total.
6 The balance sheet tells you how much money the company owes.

11.2 Complete the sentences. Look at A and B opposite to help you.

1 .... are companies that provide other companies with materials, components, etc.
2 .... are profits that the company has not distributed to shareholders.
3 .... are things a company owns and uses in its business.
4 .... consist of everything a company owes.
5 .... consists of money belonging to a company's owners.

11.3 Make word combinations using a word from each box. Then use the word combinations to complete the sentences below. Look at A and B opposite to help you.

distribute grant owe pay retain	liabilities money profits earnings credit

1 We .... a lot of our .... because we don't .... any of our .... to the shareholders.
2 Most businesses have customers who ...., because they .... them 30 or 60 days' ....
3 We have a lot of .... that we'll have to .... later this year.

"I'm afraid our accountants are being investigated for fraud – on the brighter side, our financial statements have made the New York Times best-seller fiction list."

Over to you

Look at the balance sheets of some large companies. What are the most common sub-divisions of these categories: assets, liabilities, and shareholders' equity?

12 The balance sheet 2: assets

A Fixed and current assets

MacKenzie Inc, New York Balance Sheet 31 December 20_ _	**($'000)**
Current assets	
Cash and equivalents	3,415
Accounts receivable	8,568
Inventory	5,699
Other current assets	5,562
Total current assets	23,244
Non-current assets	
Property, plant and equipment	4,500
Goodwill	950
Long-term investments	6,265
Total non-current assets	11,715
Total assets	**34,959**

In accounting, assets are generally divided into fixed and current assets. **Fixed assets** (or **non-current assets**) and investments, such as buildings and equipment, will continue to be used by the business for a long time. **Current assets** are things that will probably be used by the business in the near future. They include **cash** – money available to spend immediately, **debtors** – companies or people who owe money they will have to pay in the near future, and stock.

If a company thinks a debt will not be paid, it has to **anticipate the loss** – take action in preparation for the loss happening, according to the conservatism principle. (See Unit 7) It will **write off**, or abandon, the sum as a **bad debt**, and **make provisions** by charging a corresponding amount against profits: that is, deducting the amount of the debt from the year's profits.

B Valuation

Manufacturing companies generally have a stock of raw materials, **work-in-progress** – partially manufactured products – and products ready for sale. There are various ways of valuing stock or inventory, but generally they are valued at the **lower of cost or market**, which means whichever figure is lower: their cost – the purchase price plus the value of any work done on the items – or the current market price. This is another example of conservatism: even if the stock is expected to be sold at a profit, you should not anticipate profits.

C Tangible and intangible assets

Assets can also be classified as tangible and intangible. **Tangible assets** are assets with a physical existence – things you can touch – such as property, plant and equipment. Tangible assets are generally recorded at their historical cost (see Unit 7) less **accumulated depreciation charges** – the amount of their cost that has already been deducted from profits. This gives their **net book value.**

Intangible assets include **brand names** – legally protected names for a company's products, **patents** – exclusive rights to produce a particular new product for a fixed period, and **trade marks** – names or symbols that are put on products and cannot be used by other companies. Networks of contacts, loyal customers, reputation, trained staff or 'human capital', and skilled management can also be considered as intangible assets. Because it is difficult to give an accurate value for any of these things, companies normally only record tangible assets. For this reason, a going concern should be worth more on the stock exchange than simply its **net worth** or **net assets**: assets minus liabilities. If a company buys another one at above its net worth – because of its intangible assets – the difference in price is recorded under assets in the balance sheet as **goodwill.**

12.1 Find words and expressions in A, B and C opposite with the following meanings.

1 an amount of money that is owed but probably won't be paid
2 the accounting value of a company (assets minus liabilities)
3 a legal right to produce and sell a newly invented product for a certain period of time
4 the historical cost of an asset minus depreciation charges
5 the amount a company pays for another one, in excess of the net value of its assets
6 a legally protected word, phrase, symbol or design used to identify a product
7 to accept that a debt will not be paid
8 to deduct money from profits because of debts that will not be paid
9 products that are not complete or ready for sale
10 the amount of money owed by customers who have bought goods but not yet paid for them

12.2 Match the two parts of the sentences. Look at A, B and C opposite to help you.

1 A company's value on the stock exchange is nearly always
2 Brand names, trade marks, patents, customers, and qualified staff
3 Cash, money owed by customers, and inventory
4 Companies record inventory at the cost of buying or making the items,
5 Companies write off bad debts, and make provisions
6 Land, buildings, factories and equipment

a are current assets.
b are examples of intangible assets.
c are examples of tangible, fixed assets.
d by deducting the amount from profits.
e higher than the value of its net assets.
f or the current market price, whichever is lower.

12.3 Sort the following into current, fixed and intangible assets. Look at A and C opposite to help you.

buildings	cash in the bank	debtors
goodwill	human capital	investments
stock	land	reputation

Current assets	Fixed assets	Intangible assets
....	....	....
....	....	....
....	....	....

Over to you

Think about the company you work for, or your place of study. What are its most valuable assets? Are they shown on the balance sheet?

13 The balance sheet 3: liabilities

A Liabilities

Liabilities are amounts of money that a company owes, and are generally divided into two types – long-term and current. **Long-term liabilities** or **non-current liabilities** include bonds. (See Unit 33)

Current liabilities are expected to be paid within a year of the date of the balance sheet. They include:

- **creditors** – largely suppliers of goods or services to the business who are not paid at the time of purchase
- planned dividends
- **deferred taxes** – money that will have to be paid as tax in the future, although the payment does not have to be made now.

Current liabilities	
Short-term debt	1,555
Accounts payable	5,049
Accrued expenses	8,593
Total current liabilities	15,197
Non-current liabilities	
Deferred income taxes	950
Long-term debt	3,402
Other non-current liabilities	1,201
Total non-current liabilities	5,553
Total liabilities	**20,750**
Shareholders' equity	
Common stock	10,309
Retained earnings	3,900
Total	14,209
Total liabilities and Shareholders' equity	**34,959**

B Accrued expenses

Because of the matching principle, under which transactions and other events are reported in the periods to which they relate and not when cash is received or paid, balance sheets usually include **accrued expenses**. These are expenses that have accumulated or built up during the accounting year but will not be paid until the following year, after the date of the balance sheet. So accrued expenses are **charged against** income – that is, deducted from profits – even though the bills have not yet been received or the cash paid. Accrued expenses could include taxes and utility bills, for example electricity and water.

C Shareholders' equity on the balance sheet

Shareholders' equity is recorded on the same part of the balance sheet as liabilities, because it is money belonging to the shareholders and not the company.

Shareholders' equity includes:

- the original share capital (money from stocks or shares issued by the company: see Units 29–30)
- **share premium:** money made if the company sells shares at above their **face value** – the value written on them
- retained earnings: profits from previous years that have not been distributed to shareholders
- **reserves:** funds set aside from share capital and earnings, retained for emergencies or other future needs.

BrE: share premium;
AmE: paid-in surplus

13.1 Are the following statements true or false? Find reasons for your answers in A, B and C opposite.

1 A current liability will be paid before the date of the balance sheet.
2 A liability that must be paid in 13 months time is classified as long-term.
3 A company's accrued expenses are like money an individual saves to pay bills in the future.
4 Shareholders' equity consists of the money paid for shares, and retained earnings.
5 If companies retain part of their profits, this money no longer belongs to the owners.
6 Companies can sell shares at a higher value than the one stated on them.

13.2 Find words in A, B and C opposite with the following meanings.

1 money that will be paid in less than 12 months from the balance sheet date
2 the money that investors have paid to buy newly issued shares, minus the shares' face value
3 delayed, put off or postponed until a later time
4 built up or increased over a period of time

13.3 Sort the following into assets and liabilities. Look at A and B opposite to help you. You may need to look at Unit 12.

Accounts payable	Land and buildings
Accrued expenses	Investments
Dividends	Cash and equivalents
Inventory	Deferred taxes
Accounts receivable	Long-term debt

Assets	Liabilities
....	....
....	....
....	....
....	....
....	....

"Oh, that three billion dollars."

Over to you

Look at the last two annual reports and balance sheets of your company or one you would like to work for. What differences do you notice in the balance sheets and what reasons can you find for these?

14 The other financial statements

A The profit and loss account

Companies' annual reports contain a **profit and loss account.** This is a financial statement which shows the difference between the revenues and expenses of a period. **Non-profit** (or **not-for-profit**) **organizations** such as charities, public universities and museums generally produce an **income and expenditure account.** If they have more income than expenditure this is called a **surplus** rather than a profit.

Searby PLC

Annual Profit and Loss Account, 1/20_ _

	(£'000)
Sales Revenue	48,782
Cost of Sales	33,496
Gross Profit	15,286
Selling, General and Administrative Expenses	10,029
Earnings before Interest, Tax, Depreciation and Amortization	5,257
Depreciation and Amortization	1,368
Earnings before Interest and Tax	3,889
Interest expenses	257
Income Tax	1,064
Net Profit	2,568

At the top of these statements is total **sales revenue** or **turnover:** the total amount of money received during a specific period. Next is the **cost of sales,** also known as **cost of goods sold** (**COGS**): the costs associated with making the products that have been sold, such as raw materials, labour, and factory expenses. The difference between the sales revenue and the cost of sales is **gross profit.** There are many other costs or expenses that have to be deducted from gross profit, such as rent, electricity and office salaries. These are often grouped together as **selling, general and administrative expenses** (**SG&A**).

The statement also usually shows **EBITDA** (earnings before interest, tax, depreciation and amortization) and **EBIT** (earnings before interest and tax). The first figure is more objective because depreciation and amortization expenses can vary depending on which system a company uses.

After all the expenses and deductions is the **net profit,** often called the **bottom line.** This profit can be distributed as dividends (unless the company has to cover past losses), or transferred to reserves.

BrE: net profit; AmE: net income
BrE: profit and loss account; AmE: income statement

B The cash flow statement

British and American companies also produce a **cash flow statement.** This gives details of cash flows – money coming into and leaving the business, relating to:

- **operations** – day-to-day activities
- **investing** – buying or selling property, plant and equipment
- **financing** – issuing or repaying debt, or issuing shares.

The cash flow statement shows how effectively a company generates and manages cash. Other names are sometimes used for it, including **funds flow statement** and **source and application of funds statement.**

British companies also have to produce a **statement of total recognized gains and losses** (**STRGL**), showing any gains and losses that are not included in the profit and loss account, such as the revaluation of fixed assets.

14.1 Which figure in each of the following pairs is higher for a profitable company? Look at A opposite to help you.

1 cost of sales / sales revenue
2 gross profit / net profit
3 EBIT / EBITDA
4 net profit / pre-tax income
5 income tax / net profit

14.2 Complete the text with words from the box. You will need to use each word more than once. Look at B opposite to help you.

financing	investing	operations

(1) .... means making money by selling goods and services. (2) .... is spending cash, for the business's future growth, including cash acquired by selling assets. (3) .... involves raising money by issuing stocks and bonds (and also paying dividends and interest and repaying bonds). It is better for the company if it can pay for future growth out of money from (4) .... , without having to use (5) .... So a 'healthy' cash flow means that the amount of cash provided by (6) .... is greater than the cash used for (7) ....

14.3 Would the following appear as operating, financing or investing activities on a cash flow statement? Look at the example below to help you.

Changes in operating assets and liabilities	Payments to repurchase stock
Dividends paid	Sale of property
Purchase of plant and equipment	Depreciation and amortization expenses
Net income	Income taxes payable
Issuance of stock	Repayment of debt

Godwin-Malone Inc, New York

Cash flow statement ($'000)	**20_ _**	**20_ _**
Earnings	1,811	1,274
Amortization	924	683
Other adjustments to Earnings	33	–6
Net cash provided from operations	**2,768**	**1,951**
Proceeds from issuing new stock	234	167
Stock dividends paid	–14	
Net cash provided from financing	**220**	**167**
Additions to property, plant and equipment	–2,351	–1,755
Net cash used for investing	**–2,351**	**–1,755**
Change in cash and equivalents during year	**356**	**97**
Cash and equivalents, beginning of year	2,150	2,014
Cash and equivalents, end of year	2,506	2,111

Over to you

Look at cash flow statements in company annual reports, and at the share prices of those companies over the past years. What happened to the share price of companies that generated more cash than they spent, and what happened to those that spent more than they generated?

15 Financial ratios 1

A Types of financial ratio

Financial **ratios** express the relationships between two or more items on financial statements. They allow investors and creditors to compare a company's present situation and performance with its past performance, and with other companies. Ratios measure:

- **liquidity**: how easily a company can turn some of its assets into cash
- **solvency**: whether a company has enough cash to pay short-term debts, or whether it could **go bankrupt** – have its assets sold to repay creditors
- **efficiency**: how well a company uses its resources.

B Liquidity and solvency ratios

$$\frac{\text{current assets}}{\text{current liabilities}}$$

This is the **current ratio**, which is a calculation of current assets divided by current liabilities. It measures liquidity and shows how much of a company's assets will have to be converted into cash in the next year to pay debts. The higher the ratio, the more chance creditors have of being paid. For example, if MacKenzie Inc (see Units 12–13) has current assets of $23,244,000 and current liabilities of $15,197,000, its current ratio is 1.53, which is acceptable. It is often argued that the current ratio of a healthy company should be closer to 2.0 than 1.0, meaning that it has nearly twice as many assets as liabilities.

Suppliers granting short-term credit to a company prefer the current ratio to be high because this reduces their risk. Yet shareholders usually prefer it to be low, because this means that the company has invested its assets for the future.

$$\frac{\text{liquid assets}}{\text{current liabilities}}$$

This is the **quick ratio** or **acid test**, which is a calculation of **liquid assets** divided by current liabilities. It measures short-term solvency. Liquid assets are current assets minus stocks or inventory, as these might be difficult to sell. MacKenzie Inc's quick ratio is 1.15.

C Earnings and dividends

Shareholders are interested in ratios relating to a company's share price, earnings, and dividend payments.

$$\frac{\text{total earnings for the year}}{\text{the number of ordinary shares}}$$

This is **earnings per share** (**EPS**). It tells investors how much of the company's profit belongs to each share. If a company makes a post-tax profit of €1.5 million, and it has issued 2 million shares, EPS = €0.75.

$$\frac{\text{the market price of an ordinary share}}{\text{the past year's EPS}}$$

This is the **price/earnings ratio** or **P/E ratio.** It shows how expensive the share is. If a company has EPS of €0.75 and the share is selling for €9.00, the P/E ratio is 12 (€9 per share divided by €0.75 earnings per share = 12 P/E.) A high P/E ratio shows that investors are prepared to pay a high multiple of the earnings for a share, because they expect it to do well in the future.

$$\frac{\text{ordinary share dividend}}{\text{net profit}}$$

This is **dividend cover** or **times dividend covered,** which shows how many times the company's total annual dividends could have been paid out of its available annual earnings. If a company has EPS of 75 cents and it pays out a dividend of 30 cents, the dividend cover is 75 / 30 = 2.5. A high dividend cover shows that the company has a lot of money, but that it is not being very generous to its shareholders. A ratio of 2.0 or higher is generally considered safe (it means that the company can easily afford the dividend), but anything below 1.5 is risky. A low dividend cover – below 1.0 – means the company is paying out retained surpluses from previous years.

15.1 Find words in A opposite with the following meanings.

1 the ability to sell an asset for cash
2 how well a business uses its assets
3 the relationship between two figures
4 how easily a business can pay bills or debts when they are due

15.2 Make word combinations using a word from each box. One word can be used twice. Then use the word combinations to complete the sentences below. Look at B and C opposite to help you.

acid current dividend liquid quick	assets cover ratio test

1 .... consist of cash and things that can be easily sold and converted to cash.
2 A high .... shows that the company is retaining a lot of money belonging to its shareholders.
3 The .... or .... doesn't count stock or inventory because this might be difficult or impossible to turn into cash.
4 The .... shows a company's ability to pay its short-term debts.

15.3 Match the two parts of the sentences. Look at B and C opposite to help you.

1 If a company pays out retained surpluses from past years
2 Some investors are worried that the new stock issue
3 A high current ratio indicates short-term financial strength but
4 Wall Street is on a historic price-earnings ratio of around 35, which

a it does not measure how efficiently the company is utilizing its resources.
b its dividend cover will fall below 1.0.
c makes the market very expensive, as the long-term average is 14.45.
d will dilute the company's earnings per share.

Over to you

Look at a company's financial statements. Which of the financial ratios mentioned in this unit can be calculated:

- from the balance sheet?
- from the profit and loss account?
- using both these statements?

Which ratios require additional information?

16 Financial ratios 2

A Profitability

There are various **profitability** ratios that allow investors to compare a company's profit with its sales, its assets or its capital. Financial analysts usually include them in their reports on companies.

$$\frac{\text{gross profit (sales – cost of goods sold)}}{\text{sales}}$$

This is the **gross profit margin.** It is the money a company has left after it pays for the cost of the goods or services it has sold. A company with a higher gross profit margin than competitors in its industry is more efficient, and should be able to make a profit in the future.

$$\frac{\text{net profit}}{\text{total assets}}$$

This is **return on assets.** It measures how efficiently the firm's assets are being used to generate profits.

$$\frac{\text{net profit}}{\text{shareholders' equity}}$$

This is **return on equity** (**ROE**). It shows how big a company's profit is (after interest and tax) compared with the shareholders' equity or funds.

B Leverage

$$\frac{\text{debt}}{\text{shareholders' equity}}$$

This is **gearing** or **leverage**, often expressed as a percentage. It shows how far a company is funded by loans rather than its own capital. A **highly geared** or **highly leveraged** company is one that has a lot of debt compared to equity.

$$\frac{\text{EBIT (see Unit 14)}}{\text{interest charges}}$$

This is **interest cover** or **times interest earned.** It compares a business's annual interest payments with its earnings before interest and tax, and shows how easily the company can pay long-term debt costs. A low interest cover (e.g. below 1.0) shows that a business is having difficulties generating the cash necessary for its interest payments.

BrE: gearing;
AmE: leverage

Citigroup Inc Key Ratios, 2005

	Citigroup	Banking Industry Average	S&P 500 Average
Growth Rates %			
Sales	11.5	29.4	10.7
EPS	3.2	21.2	11.2
Price Ratio			
P/E Ratio	13.9	14.5	20.6
Profit Margins			
Pre-Tax Margin	21.8	23.7	47.3
Net Profit Margin	15.5	16.3	7.6
Financial Condition			
Debt/Equity Ratio	1.9	1.32	1.1
Interest Cover	2.0	2.1	3.4
Investment Returns %			
Return On Equity	15.7	13.2	14.5
Return On Assets	1.2	1.0	2.5

16.1 Match the two parts of the sentences. Look at A and B opposite to help you.

1 After borrowing millions to finance the takeover of a rival firm, the company's
2 Although sales fell 5%, the company's
3 Like profit growth, return on equity is a measure of
4 With just 24% gearing, the company can afford

a gross profit margin rose 9% from a year ago, so senior management isn't worried.
b how good a company is at making money.
c interest cover is the lowest it has ever been.
d to acquire its rival, which would help to increase its steady growth.

16.2 Read the text and answer the questions below. You may need to look at Units 11–14.

Predicting insolvency: the Altman Z-Score

The Z-Score was created by Edward Altman in the 1960s. It combines a set of 5 financial ratios and a weighting system to predict a company's probability of failure using 8 variables from its financial statements.

The ratios are multiplied by their weights, and the results are added together.

The 5 financial ratios and their weight factors are:

A	EBIT / Total Assets	× 3.3
B	Net Sales / Total Assets	× 0.999
C	Market Value of Equity / Total Liabilities	× 0.6
D	Working Capital / Total Assets	× 1.2
E	Retained Earnings / Total Assets	× 1.4

Therefore the Z-Score = A × 3.3 + B × 0.999 + C × 0.6 + D × 1.2 + E × 1.4

Interpreting the Z-Score

> 3.0	– based on these financial figures, the company is safe
2.7–2.99	– insolvency is possible
1.8–2.7	– there is a good chance of the company going bankrupt within 2 years
< 1.80	– there is a very high probability of the company going bankrupt

Which ratio in the Z-Score takes into account:

1 money used for everyday expenses?
2 undistributed profits belonging to the shareholders?
3 income or earnings before interest and tax are deducted?
4 the current share price?
5 the amount of money received from selling goods or services?

Over to you

Look at the financial statements of a company you are interested in and calculate the company's Z-Score. Is it in good financial health?

17 Cost accounting

A Direct and indirect costs

Cost accounting involves calculating the costs of different products or services, so that company managers can know what price to charge for particular products and services and which are the most **profitable. Direct costs** – those that can be directly related to the production of particular units of a product – are quite easy to calculate. Examples include manufacturing materials and manufacturing wages. But there are also **indirect costs** or **overheads** – costs and expenses that cannot be identified with particular manufacturing processes or units of production. Examples include rent or property taxes for the company's offices and factories, electricity for lighting and heating, the maintenance department, the factory canteen or restaurant, managers' salaries, and so on. Costs such as these are often grouped together on the profit and loss account or income statement as Selling, General and Administrative Expenses.

BrE: overheads;
AmE: overhead

B Fixed and variable costs

Companies also differentiate between fixed costs and variable costs. **Fixed costs** are those that do not change in the short term, even if the production level changes, such as rent and interest payments. **Variable costs** are those that change in proportion to the volume of production, such as components and raw materials, and overtime payments.

Manufacturing companies have to find a way of **allocating** fixed and variable costs to the various products they make: that is, they divide up the costs and charge them to the different products. **Absorption costing** attempts to charge all direct costs and all production costs, and sometimes all indirect costs such as administrative expenses, to each of the company's products or services. **Activity-based costing** calculates all the costs connected with a particular activity (e.g. product design, manufacturing, distribution, customer service), even if they are carried out by different departments in the company. Most companies have departments or functions that do not generate any profit but only incur costs (e.g. accounting and legal departments). For accounting purposes, companies often make these departments into **cost centres**, and allocate or charge all the costs related to them separately.

BrE: cost centre;
AmE: cost center

C Breakeven analysis

When deciding whether it would be profitable to produce a product, or offer a service, companies do a **breakeven analysis**. This compares expected sales of the new product with expected costs – both direct and indirect – at various production levels. The **breakeven point** is the **sales volume** – the number of units sold – at which the company **covers its costs** – pays all its expenses. To make a profit, it is necessary to sell more than this.

Although cost accounting allows companies to calculate production costs, pricing decisions also depend on:

- the level of demand
- the prices of competitors' products
- the company's financial situation
- the company's **objectives** – the goals or aims it wants to accomplish
- the company's **marketing policies** – whether it is interested in maximizing sales or maximizing profit.

17.1 Match the words in the box with the definitions below. Look at A, B and C opposite to help you.

breakeven point	cost centre	fixed costs
overheads	variable costs	profitable

1 expenses that are not clearly related to production or manufacturing
2 a unit of activity in an organization for which costs are calculated separately
3 costs that depend on the amount produced
4 adjective meaning providing income for a company
5 costs that do not change according to the production volume
6 the sales volume at which a company doesn't make a loss, but doesn't make a profit

17.2 Sort the following into direct, indirect, fixed and variable costs. Look at A and B opposite to help you.

Cost	Direct	Indirect	Fixed	Variable
Advertising expenses				
Bad debts		✓		✓
Components	✓			✓
Electricity to run machines				
Electricity for heating				
Equipment repairs				
Factory canteen				
Overtime pay				
Raw materials				
Property tax				
Rent				

17.3 Which of the following statements describes:

1 absorption costing?
2 activity-based costing?

a As well as direct manufacturing costs – materials and labour – we allocate part of our fixed and variable manufacturing overheads to the cost of every product.

b We identify all the different functions within the company, and assign costs to products and services according to how much these functions are involved in the process of providing the products and services.

Over to you

What do you think were the most important factors in the pricing of:

- this book?
- two other products you bought recently?

18 Pricing

A Manufacturers' pricing strategies

These are a student's notes from a lecture about pricing.

- Companies' **prices** are influenced by production and distribution costs, both **direct** and **indirect**.
- **Mark-up** or **cost-plus pricing**: some firms just calculate the **unit cost** and add a percentage.
- Most companies consider other factors, like demand, competitors' prices, **sales targets** and **profit targets**.
- **Market penetration pricing**: some companies **launch** products at a price that only gives them a very small profit, because they want a big **market share**. This allows them to make profits later because of **economies of scale**, e.g. Bic pens, lighters and razors; Dell PCs.
- **Market skimming**: some customers will pay almost any price, e.g. for a new hi-tech product, so the company can charge a really high price, then lower it to reach other **market segments**, e.g. Intel with new microchips.
- If a company has a higher demand for its products than it's able to supply, it can raise its prices. This is often done by **monopolists**.
- **Prestige pricing** or **image pricing**: products positioned at the luxury end of a market *need* to have a high price: the **target customers** probably won't buy them if they think the price is too low, e.g. BMW, Rolex.
- **Going-rate pricing**: if a product is almost identical to competitors' products, companies might charge the same price.

unit cost: the expenses involved in producing each individual product

sales target/profit target: the quantity of sales/profit a business wants to achieve

launch: to introduce a product onto the market

market share: the proportion of total sales in the market

economies of scale: the cost of producing each unit decreases as the volume of production increases

market segments: groups of consumers with similar needs and wants

monopolists: companies that are the only supplier of a product or service

target customers: the customers whose needs the company wants to satisfy

B Retail pricing strategies

- **Loss-leader pricing**: retailers (e.g. supermarkets) often offer some items at a very low price that isn't profitable, to attract customers who then buy more products which *are* profitable.
- **Odd pricing** or **odd-even pricing**: many producers and retailers believe a customer sees a price of €29.95 as in the €20 price range rather than the €30 one.
- **Elasticity**: demand is **elastic** if sales respond directly to **price variations** – e.g. if the price is cut, sales increase. If sales remain the same after a change in price, demand is **inelastic**.

18.1 Find five verbs in A and B opposite that can be used to make word combinations with 'prices'. Then use the verbs to complete the sentences below.

....
....
.... **prices**
....
....

1 Economists say that if sales increase when you .... a price, demand is elastic.
2 If we have more customers than products available, we generally .... our prices.
3 Luxury goods companies make huge profits, because their customers are prepared to .... really high prices.
4 Our product's really the same as our competitors', so we'll probably .... the same price.
5 After we've skimmed the market, we can .... the price to get more customers.

18.2 Match the pricing strategies in the box with the statements below. Look at A and B opposite to help you.

going-rate pricing	loss-leader pricing	market penetration	market skimming
mark-up pricing	odd pricing	prestige pricing	

1 Because of our famous brand name and our reputation for quality, we can charge a *very* high price.

2 We never use whole numbers like \$10 or \$20. Our prices always end in 95 or 99 cents.

3 We launch our products at high prices, and then reduce them a few months later to get more customers.

4 We just get the cost accountants to work out how much it costs to make the product, and add our profit.

5 Demand isn't very elastic, so we charge the same price as our main competitors.

6 We actually sell a few products at breakeven price, but this brings in customers who also buy a lot of other things.

7 We charge a really low price at first, because we want to sell as many units of the product as possible.

Over to you

Can you think of at least one producer or retailer that uses each of the pricing strategies mentioned here?

19 Personal banking

A Current accounts

A **current account** is an account which allows customers to take out or **withdraw** money, with no restrictions. Money in the account does not usually earn a high rate of **interest**: the bank does not pay much for 'borrowing' your money. However, many people also have a **savings account** or **deposit account** which pays more interest but has restrictions on when you can withdraw your money. Banks usually send monthly **statements** listing recent sums of money going out, called **debits**, and sums of money coming in, called **credits**.

Nearly all customers have a **debit card** allowing them to make **withdrawals** and do other transactions at **cash dispensers**. Most customers have a **credit card** which can be used for buying goods and services as well as for borrowing money. In some countries, people pay bills with **cheques**. In other countries, banks don't issue chequebooks and people pay bills by **bank transfer**. These include **standing orders**, which are used to pay regular fixed sums of money, and **direct debits**, which are used when the amount and payment date varies.

BrE: current account; AmE: checking account
BrE: cash dispenser, cash machine; AmE: ATM (Automated Teller Machine)
BrE: cheque; AmE: check

B Banking products and services

Commercial banks offer **loans** – fixed sums of money that are lent for a fixed period (e.g. two years). They also offer **overdrafts**, which allow customers to **overdraw** an account – they can have a debt, up to an agreed limit, on which interest is calculated daily. This is cheaper than a loan if, for example, you only need to overdraw for a short period. Banks also offer **mortgages** to people who want to buy a place to live. These are long-term loans on which the property acts as **collateral** or a guarantee for the bank. If the borrower doesn't repay the mortgage, the bank can **repossess** the house or flat – the bank takes it back from the buyer, and sells it.

Banks exchange **foreign currency** for people going abroad, and sell **traveller's cheques** which are protected against loss or theft. They also offer advice about **investments** and **private pension plans** – saving money for when you retire from work. Increasingly, banks also try to sell insurance products to their customers.

BrE: traveller's cheque; AmE: traveler's check

C E-banking

In the 1990s, many commercial banks thought the future would be in **telephone banking** and **internet banking** or **e-banking**. But they discovered that most of their customers preferred to go to **branches** – local offices of the bank – especially ones that had longer opening hours, and which were conveniently situated in shopping centres.

BrE: shopping centre; AmE: shopping mall

19.1 Complete the advertisement with words from the box. Look at A and B opposite to help you.

credit card	current accounts	debit card
direct debit	statements	foreign currency
savings accounts	standing order	traveller's cheques

Calling all students!

ABC Bank now offers 1% interest on (1) .... and 2.5% on (2) .... We will give you a chequebook and plastic: a free (3) .... for use in cash dispensers, and the possibility to apply for a (4) .... You can pay fixed monthly bills by (5) .... , and other bills by (6) .... There are no account charges as long as you remain in credit, and we send you free monthly (7) .... We can also sell you (8) .... for your next holiday, or (9) .... for greater security. What are you waiting for? Call us today.

19.2 Find words in B opposite with the following meanings.

1 what you can earn when you leave your money in the bank
2 an amount of money borrowed from a bank for a certain length of time, usually for a specific purpose
3 something that acts as a security or a guarantee for a debt
4 an arrangement to withdraw more money from a bank account than you have placed in it
5 a long-term loan to buy somewhere to live
6 an arrangement for saving money to give you an income when you stop working
7 to take back property that has not been completely paid for

19.3 Are the following statements true or false? Find reasons for your answers in A, B and C opposite.

1 Current accounts pay more interest than savings accounts.
2 There is less risk for a bank with a mortgage than with unsecured loans without collateral.
3 Traveller's cheques are safer for tourists than carrying foreign currency.
4 The majority of customers prefer to do their personal banking at the bank.
5 Bank branches are now all in shopping centres.

Over to you

Do you prefer to go to the local branch of your bank, or to use the internet or the telephone? Why? Why do you think most customers still prefer to go to the bank?

20 Commercial and retail banking

A Commercial and retail banks

When people have more money than they need to spend, they may choose to **save** it. They **deposit** it in a **bank account**, at a **commercial** or **retail bank**, and the bank generally **pays interest** to the **depositors**. The bank then uses the money that has been deposited to **grant loans** – lend money to **borrowers** who need more money than they have available. Banks make a profit by charging a higher rate of interest to borrowers than they pay to depositors.

Commercial banks can also move or **transfer** money from one customer's bank account to another one, at the same or another bank, when the customer asks them to.

B Credit

Banks also **create credit** – make money available for someone to borrow – because the money they lend, from their deposits, is usually spent and so transferred to another bank account.

The capital a bank has and the loans it has made are its **assets**. The customers' deposits are **liabilities** because the money is owed to someone else. Banks have to keep a certain percentage of their assets as **reserves** for borrowers who want to withdraw their money. This is known as the **reserve requirement**. For example, if the reserve requirement is 10%, a bank that receives a €100 deposit can lend €90 of it. If the borrower spends the money and writes a cheque to someone who deposits the €90, the bank receiving that deposit can lend €81. As the process continues, the banking system can expand the first deposit of €100 into nearly €1,000. In this way, it creates credit of almost €900.

C Loans and risks

Before lending money, a bank has to **assess** or calculate the risk involved. Generally, the greater the risk for the bank of not being repaid, the higher the interest rate they charge. Most retail banks have **standardized** products for **personal customers**, such as **personal loans**. This means that all customers who have been granted a loan have the same **terms and conditions** – they have the same rules for paying back the money.

Banks have more complicated **risk assessment** methods for **corporate customers** – business clients – but large companies these days prefer to raise their own finance rather than borrow from banks.

Banks have to find a balance between **liquidity** – having cash available when depositors want it – and different **maturities** – dates when loans will be repaid. They also have to balance **yield** – how much money a loan pays – and risk.

20.1 Complete the sentences from banks' websites. Look at A and C opposite to help you.

1 If you need instant access to all your money, this is the .... for you.

2 Our products for .... include business overdrafts, loan repayments that reflect your cash flow, and commercial mortgages.

3 Our local branch managers are encouraged to help local businesses and are authorized to .... and overdrafts.

4 We offer standardized loans: you can be sure you won't get less favourable terms and .... than our other ....

20.2 Match the two parts of the sentences. Look at A, B and C opposite to help you.

1 Banks lend savers' deposits
2 They also create credit by
3 How much credit banks can create
4 Before lending money,
5 The interest rate on a loan
6 Banks always need liquidity,

a banks have to assess the risk involved.
b depends on the reserve requirements.
c depends on how risky it is for the bank to lend the money.
d so they can't lend all their money in loans with long maturities.
e lending the same original deposit several times.
f to people who need to borrow money.

20.3 Find verbs in A, B and C opposite that can be used to make word combinations with the nouns below. Then use some of the verbs to complete the sentences.

.... / .... **interest**

.... / .... **risks**

.... / .... **money**

1 With standardized products, all customers are .... the same interest rate.
2 Banks generally know from experience how much cash to keep in their reserves for customers who want to .... it.
3 Banks carefully study the financial situation of a company to .... the risk involved in lending it money.

Over to you

Look at some commercial bank websites from your country. Which bank offers the best rates to borrowers and lenders?

21 Financial institutions

A Types of financial institution

These are a student's notes from a lecture about banking.

For most of the 20th century, most banks operated in one country only (in the US, in one state only). Different kinds of banks did specialized kinds of financial business:

- Retail banks or commercial banks worked with individuals and small companies:
  - received deposits
  - made loans. (See Unit 20)
- **Investment banks** worked with big companies:
  - gave financial advice
  - **raised capital** – **increased** the amount of money companies had by **issuing stocks** or **shares** and **bonds**
  - organized **mergers** and **takeover bids**.
- **Insurance companies**
  - provided life insurance and pensions.
- **Building societies**
  - specialized in mortgages. Many have now become normal commercial banks.

bonds: debts that pay interest and are repaid at a fixed future date (see Unit 33)

merger: when two or more companies join together (see Unit 39)

takeover bid: when one company offers to **acquire** or buy another one (see Unit 39)

stocks or shares: certificates representing one unit of ownership of a company (see Unit 29)

BrE: merchant bank; AmE: investment bank
BrE: retail bank, commercial bank, High Street bank; AmE: retail bank, commercial bank
BrE: building societies; AmE: savings and loans associations

B Deregulation

The financial industry changed radically in 1980s and 90s when it was **deregulated**.

- Before **deregulation**: rules and regulations in the US, Britain and Japan prevented commercial banks doing investment banking business. Some other countries (Germany, Switzerland) already had universal banks doing all kinds of financial business.
- Today: many large international **conglomerates** offer a complete range of financial services. Individuals and companies can use a single financial institution for all their financial needs.

deregulated: there are now fewer restrictions and regulations than before

conglomerates: companies formed by mergers and takeovers (see Unit 40)

C Specialized banks

Other types of banks still have specialized functions:

- **central banks** issue currency and carry out the government's financial policy
- **private banks** manage the assets of rich people or **high net worth individuals**
- **clearing banks** pass cheques and other payments through the banking system
- **non-bank financial intermediaries** such as car manufacturers, food retailers and department stores now offer products like personal loans, credit cards and insurance.

21.1 Find words in A and B opposite with the following meanings.

1 a company offering financial services
2 the money a company uses, raised by way of shares and bonds
3 when two formerly separate companies agree to join together
4 a company formed by the merger or takeover of several other companies
5 the ending of some rules and restrictions
6 when a company offers to buy the shares of another company to gain control of it

21.2 Before financial deregulation, which types of financial institutions did these types of business? Look at A opposite to help you.

1 arranging mergers
2 offering life insurance
3 issuing shares and bonds
4 providing mortgages
5 receiving deposits and making loans to individuals and small companies
6 giving financial advice to companies
7 organizing (or defending against) takeover bids
8 providing pensions

21.3 The extracts below are from websites. Which types of banks do the websites belong to? Look at A and C opposite to help you.

1 The Federal Reserve was founded by Congress in 1913 to provide the nation with a safer, more flexible, and more stable monetary and financial system.

2 We provide a full range of products and services, including advising on corporate strategy and structure, and raising capital in equity and debt markets.

3 How can we help you? We can:
Build a long-term, one-to-one relationship with your banker.
Manage your family's diverse business and personal assets.
Build a portfolio tailored to your family's unique needs.
Play an active role in managing your assets.

4 Nearly twelve million cheques and credits pass through the system each working day. Cheque volumes reached a peak in 1990 but usage has fallen since then, mainly owing to increased use of plastic cards and direct debits by personal customers.

5 Why bank with us? Because we offer:
- a comprehensive range of accounts and services
- over 1,600 branches, many with Saturday opening
- free withdrawals from over 31,000 cash machines
- online and telephone banking for round-the-clock access to your accounts

Over to you

Does your company use more than one bank? Do you? Why?

22 Investment banking

A Raising capital

Ruth Henly works in an investment bank in New York.

'Unlike commercial banks, investment banks like ours don't lend money. Instead we act as **intermediaries** between companies and investors. We help companies and governments raise capital by **issuing securities** such as stocks and bonds – that is, we offer them for sale. We often **underwrite** securities issues: in other words, we guarantee to buy the securities ourselves if we can't find other purchasers.

As well as **initial public offerings** (**IPOs**), when companies offer stock for sale for the first time, there are other occasions when they **raise funds**. For example, they might want to expand their operations, or to **acquire** another company, or to reduce their amount of debt, or to finance a specific project. They don't only raise capital from the public: they can sell stocks or shares to **institutional investors** like insurance companies, **investment funds** – companies that invest the money of lots of small investors, and **pension funds** – companies that invest money that will later be paid to retired workers.

We also have a **stockbroking** and **dealing** department. This **executes orders** – buys and sells stocks for clients – which is broking, and trades with our own money, which is dealing. The stockbroking department also offers advice to investors.'

BrE: flotation; AmE: initial public offering (IPO)

B Mergers and acquisitions

'Investment banks often represent firms in **mergers** and **acquisitions** (see Unit 21), and **divestitures**. A divestiture is when a company sells a **subsidiary** – another company that it owns. Most of the **fee** – the money the company pays us for the service – will depend on us completing the deal successfully. This gives the bank a good reason to make sure that the transaction succeeds.'

C Consulting and research

'Large corporations have their own finance and corporate development departments. But they often use an investment bank like ours because, like a **consulting firm**, we can offer independent advice, and we have a lot of experience in financial transactions. We also have a large network of contacts, and relationships with investors and companies that could be interested in a merger or acquisition.

If we've worked on a transaction with a company, we know a lot about its business. This means we can give advice about **strategic planning** – deciding what do to in the future – or **financial restructuring** – changing the way the business is financed. Large investment banks also have extensive **research** departments with **analysts** and **forecasters** who specialize in the **valuation** of different markets, industries, companies, securities and currencies. Analysts try to work out how much things are worth now, and forecasters study the prospects for the future.'

22.1 Complete the table with words from A, B and C opposite and related forms. Put a stress mark in front of the stressed syllable in each word. The first one has been done for you.

Verb	Noun(s)	Noun for people	Adjective(s)
a'cquire		–	–
advise			–
			analytical
institute		–	
invest			–
value		–	

22.2 Complete the sentences from newspaper articles with words from the box.

acquiring	advised	divesting	fees	IPOs	merged	underwritten

1 Deutsche Telekom's IPO was .... by Goldman Sachs.

2 During their acquisition of Mannesman, Vodafone were .... by UBS.

3 Large multinationals are always .... less successful parts of their business as well as .... successful companies.

4 Big Wall Street banks earned millions of dollars in consulting .... from Enron before the company collapsed.

5 When Mitsubishi Tokyo Financial Group .... with UFJ Holdings, they became the world's biggest bank.

6 In 2000, the global value of .... was over $220 billion.

22.3 Match the words in the box with the definitions below. Look at A, B and C opposite to help you.

financial restructuring	consulting firm	forecasters	institutional investor
strategic planning	pension fund	subsidiary	valuation

1 a company of experts providing professional advice to businesses for a fee
2 a financial institution that invests money to provide retirement income for employees
3 deciding what a company is going to do in the future
4 people who try to predict what will happen in the future
5 a company that is partly or wholly owned by another one
6 a financial institution that purchases securities
7 making changes to how a company is financed
8 establishing how much something is worth

Over to you

Can you name the largest investment banks in your country? Are they local or international? Describe the services they offer.

23 Central banking

A The functions of central banks

A journalist is interviewing Professor John Webb, an expert in central banking.

What are the main functions of central banks?

Well, most countries have a central bank that provides financial services to the government and to the banking system. If a group of countries have a common currency, for example the euro, they also share a central bank, such as the European Central Bank in Frankfurt.

Some central banks are responsible for **monetary policy** – trying to control the rate of inflation to maintain **financial stability**. This involves changing interest rates. The aim is to protect the value of the currency – what it will purchase at home and in other currencies.

In many countries, the central bank **supervises** and **regulates** the banking system and the whole financial sector. It also collects financial data and publishes statistics, and provides financial information for consumers. In most countries, the central bank prints and **issues currency** – putting banknotes into circulation. It also participates in clearing cheques (see Unit 21) and settling debts among commercial banks.

B The central bank and the commercial banks

How exactly does the central bank supervise the commercial banks?

Well, commercial banks have to keep reserves – a certain amount of their deposits – for customers who want to withdraw their money. These are held by the central bank, which can also change the **reserve–asset ratio** – the minimum percentage of its deposits a bank has to keep in its reserves.

If one bank goes bankrupt, it can quickly affect the stability of the whole **financial system**. And if depositors think a bank is unsafe they might all try to withdraw their money. If this happens it's called a **bank run** or a **run on the bank**, and the bank will quickly use up its reserves. Central banks can act as **lender of last resort**, which means lending money to financial institutions in difficulty, to allow them to make payments. But central banks don't always **bail out** or rescue banks in difficulty, because this could lead banks to take risks that are too big.

C Central banks and exchange rates

What about exchange rates with foreign currencies?

Central banks manage a country's reserves of **gold** and foreign currencies. They can try to have an influence on the **exchange rate** – the price at which their currency can be converted into other currencies. They do this by **intervening** on the **currency markets**, and moving the rate up or down by buying or selling their currency. (See Unit 44) This changes the balance of **supply** – how much is being sold – and **demand** – how much is being bought.

23.1 Match the two parts of the sentences. Look at A and B opposite to help you.

1 The central bank will sometimes lend money
2 Banks would probably start taking too many risks
3 Central banks are usually responsible for
4 The central bank can alter
5 There will be low and stable inflation

a if they could always be sure of rescue by the central bank.
b if there is a run on a commercial bank.
c if monetary policy is successful.
d printing and distributing banknotes.
e the amount of money commercial banks are able to lend.

23.2 Complete the text from the website of the Federal Reserve, the central bank of the United States. Look at A opposite to help you.

Today the Federal Reserve's duties fall into four general areas:

➤ conducting the nation's (a) .... policy;
➤ (b) .... and regulating banking institutions and protecting the credit rights of consumers;
➤ maintaining the (c) .... of the financial system; and
➤ providing certain (d) .... services to the US government, the public, financial institutions, and foreign official institutions.

23.3 Make word combinations using a word from each box. One word can be used twice. Then use the word combinations to complete the sentences below. Look at A, B and C opposite to help you.

bank currency exchange financial monetary	markets run system policy rate stability

1 ...., including setting interest rates, is designed to maintain ....
2 If there's a .... and the bank goes bankrupt, this can have a rapid effect on the whole ....
3 On one day in 1992, the Bank of England lost over £1 billion (more than half of the country's foreign reserves) in the ...., trying to protect the .... of the pound.

Over to you

Is the central bank in your country independent from the government? What powers and responsibilities does it have?

24 Interest rates

A Interest rates and monetary policy

An **interest rate** is the cost of borrowing money: the percentage of the amount of a loan paid by the borrower to the lender for the use of the lender's money. A country's minimum interest rate (the lowest rate that any lender can charge) is usually set by the central bank, as part of monetary policy, designed to keep inflation low. This can be achieved if demand (for goods and services, and the money with which to buy them) is nearly the same as supply. Demand is how much people consume and businesses **invest** in factories, machinery, creating new jobs, etc. Supply is the creation of goods and services, using **labour** – paid work – and capital. When interest rates fall, people borrow more, and spend rather than **save**, and companies invest more. Consequently, the level of demand rises. When interest rates rise, so that borrowing becomes more expensive, individuals tend to save more and consume less. Companies also invest less, so demand is reduced.

If interest rates are set too low, the demand for goods and services grows faster than the market's ability to supply them. This causes prices to rise so that inflation occurs. If interest rates are set too high, this lowers borrowing and spending. This brings down inflation, but also reduces **output** – the amount of goods produced and services performed, and **employment** – the number of jobs in the country.

BrE: labour; AmE: labor

B Different interest rates

The **discount rate** is the rate that the central bank sets to lend short-term funds to commercial banks. When this rate changes, the commercial banks change their own **base rate**, the rate they charge their most reliable customers like large corporations. This is the rate from which they calculate all their other deposit and lending rates for savers and borrowers.

Banks make their profits from the difference, known as a **margin** or **spread**, between the interest rates they charge borrowers and the rates they pay to depositors. The rate that borrowers pay depends on their **creditworthiness**, also known as **credit standing** or **credit rating**. This is the lender's estimation of a borrower's present and future **solvency**: their ability to pay debts. The higher the borrower's solvency, the lower the interest rate they pay. Borrowers can usually get a lower interest rate if the loan is guaranteed by securities or other collateral. For example, **mortgages** for which a house or apartment is collateral are usually cheaper than ordinary bank loans or **overdrafts** – arrangements to borrow by spending more than is in your bank account. Long-term loans such as mortgages often have **floating** or **variable interest rates** that change according to the supply and demand for money.

Leasing or **hire purchase** (**HP**) agreements have higher interest rates than bank loans and overdrafts. These are when a consumer makes a series of monthly payments to buy durable goods (e.g. a car, furniture). Until the goods are paid for, the buyer is only hiring or renting them, and they belong to the lender. The interest rate is high as there is little security for the lender: the goods could easily become damaged.

BrE: base rate; AmE: prime rate

"On this model there's a sensory device that prevents you from starting, unless your seat belts are fastened and your HP repayments are up to date."

24.1 Match the words in the box with the definitions below. Look at A and B opposite to help you.

creditworthy	floating rate	invest	labour
spread	output	solvency	interest rate

1 the cost of borrowing money, expressed as a percentage of the loan
2 having sufficient cash available when debts have to be paid
3 paid work that provides goods and services
4 a borrowing rate that isn't fixed
5 safe to lend money to
6 the difference between borrowing and lending rates
7 the quantity of goods and services produced in an economy
8 to spend money in order to produce income or profits

24.2 Name the interest rates and loans. Then put them in order, from the lowest rate to the highest. Look at B opposite to help you.

a ....: a loan to buy property (a house, flat, etc.)
b ....: borrowing money to buy something like a car, spreading payment over 36 months
c ....: commercial banks' lending rate for their most secure customers
d ....: occasionally borrowing money by spending more than you have in the bank
e ....: the rate at which central banks make secured loans to commercial banks

1		2		3		4		5	

lowest — highest

24.3 Are the following statements true or false? Find reasons for your answers in A and B opposite.

1 All interest rates are set by central banks.
2 When interest rates fall, people tend to spend and borrow more.
3 A borrower who is very solvent will pay a very high interest rate.
4 Loans are usually cheaper if they are guaranteed by some form of security or collateral.
5 If banks make loans to customers with a lower level of solvency, they can increase their margins.
6 One of the causes of changes in interest rates is the supply and demand for money.

Over to you

What are the average interest rates paid to depositors by banks in your country? How much do borrowers have to pay for loans, overdrafts, mortgages and credit card debts? Is there much difference among competing banks?

25 Money markets

A The money markets

The **money markets** consist of a network of corporations, financial institutions, investors and governments, which need to borrow or invest **short-term** capital (up to 12 months). For example, a business or government that needs cash for a few weeks only can use the money market. So can a bank that wants to invest money that depositors could withdraw at any time. Through the money markets, borrowers can find short-term **liquidity** by turning assets into cash. They can also deal with irregular **cash flows** – in-comings and out-goings of money – more cheaply than borrowing from a commercial bank. Similarly, investors can make short-term deposits with investment companies at **competitive** interest rates: higher ones than they would get from a bank. Borrowers and lenders in the money markets use banks and **investment companies** whose business is trading **financial instruments** such as stocks, bonds, short-term loans and debts, rather than lending money.

B Common money market instruments

- **Treasury bills** (or **T-bills**) are bonds issued by governments. The most common **maturity** – the length of time before a bond becomes repayable – is three months, although they can have a maturity of up to one year. T-bills in a country's own currency are generally the safest possible investment. They are usually sold at a **discount** from their **nominal value** – the value written on them – rather than paying interest. For example, a T-bill can be sold at 99% of the value written on it, and **redeemed** or paid back at 100% at maturity, three months later.
- **Commercial paper** is a short-term loan issued by major companies, also sold at a discount. It is **unsecured**, which means it is not guaranteed by the company's assets.
- **Certificates of deposit** (or **CDs**) are short- or medium-term, interest-paying **debt instruments** – written promises to repay a debt. They are issued by banks to large depositors who can then trade them in the short-term money markets. They are known as **time deposits**, because the holder agrees to lend the money – by buying the certificate – for a specified amount of time.

Note: **Nominal value** is also called **par value** or **face value**.

C Repos

Another very common form of financial contract is a **repurchase agreement** (or **repo**). A repo is a combination of two transactions, as shown below. The dealer hopes to find a long-term buyer for the securities before repurchasing them.

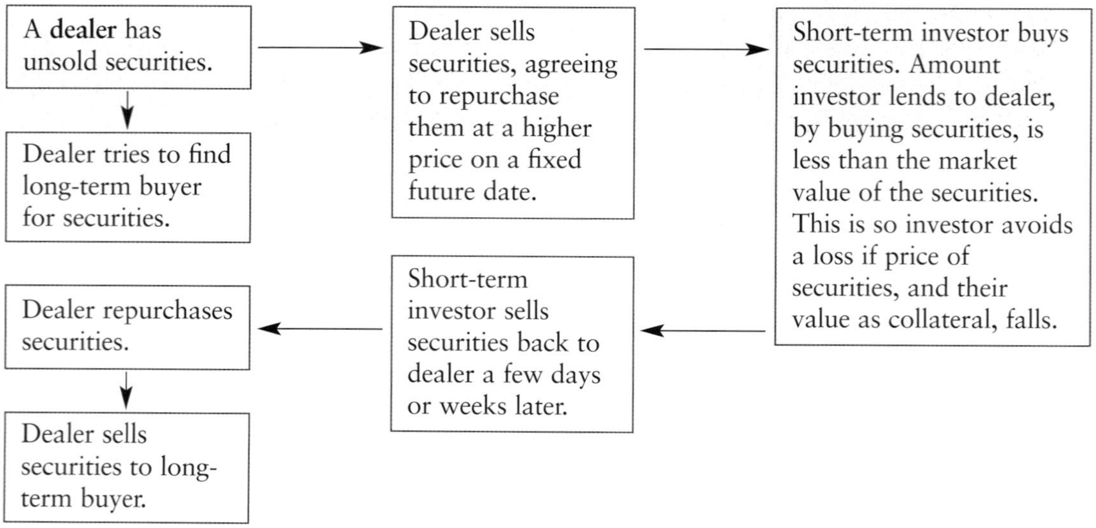

25.1 Are the following statements true or false? Find reasons for your answers in A and B opposite.

1 Organizations use the money markets as an alternative to borrowing from banks.
2 Money markets are a source of long-term finance.
3 All money market instruments pay interest.
4 Certificates of deposit are issued by major manufacturing companies.
5 Commercial paper is guaranteed by the government.
6 Some money market instruments can have more than one owner before they mature.

25.2 Match the words in the box with the definitions below. Look at A and B opposite to help you.

cash flow	competitive	discount
liquidity	maturity	par value
redeemed	short-term	unsecured

1 a price below the usual or advertised price
2 adjective describing a good price, compared to others on the market
3 the ability to sell an asset quickly for cash
4 (in finance) adjective meaning up to one year
5 adjective meaning with no guarantee or collateral
6 repaid
7 the length of time before a bond has to be repaid
8 the movement of money in and out of an organization
9 the price written on a security

25.3 Match the two parts of the sentences. Look at B and C opposite to help you.

1 Most money market securities
2 A treasury bill is safe because it
3 Commercial paper
4 Certificates of deposit (CDs)
5 Repurchase agreements (repos)

a is issued by corporations, so it is riskier than T-bills.
b are short-term, liquid, safe, and sold at a discount.
c is guaranteed by the government.
d are short-term exchanges of cash for securities.
e are issued to holders of time deposits in a bank.

Over to you

What kind of money market instruments are you familiar with? Which ones would be most useful for your company, or for a company you would like to work for?

26 Islamic banking

A Interest-free banking

Some financial institutions do not charge interest on loans or pay interest on savings, because it is against certain ethical or religious beliefs. For example, in Islamic countries and major financial centres there are Islamic banks that offer **interest-free** banking.

Islamic banks do not pay interest to depositors or charge interest to borrowers. Instead they invest in companies and share the profits with their depositors. Investment financing and trade financing are done on a **profit and loss sharing** (**PLS**) basis. Consequently the banks, their depositors, and their borrowers also share the risks of the business. This form of financing is similar to that of **venture capitalists** or **risk capitalists** who buy the shares of new companies. (See Unit 28)

B Types of accounts

Current accounts in Islamic banks give no return – pay no interest – to depositors. They are a **safekeeping** arrangement between the depositors and the bank, which allows the depositors to withdraw their money at any time, and permits the bank to use this money. Islamic banks do not usually grant overdrafts on current accounts. Savings accounts can pay a return to depositors, depending on the bank's **profitability**: that is, its ability to earn a profit. Therefore the amount of return depends on how much profit the bank makes in a given period. However, these payments are not guaranteed. There is no fixed **rate of return**: the amount of money the investment pays, expressed as a percentage of the amount invested, is not fixed. Banks are careful to invest money from savings accounts in relatively risk-free, short-term projects. **Investment accounts** are **fixed-term** deposits which cannot be withdrawn before maturity. They receive a share of the bank's profits. In theory, the rate of return could be negative, if the bank makes a loss. In other words, the capital is not guaranteed.

C Leasing and short-term loans

To finance the purchase of expensive consumer goods for personal consumption, Islamic banks can buy an item for a customer, and the customer repays the bank at a higher price later on. Or the bank can buy an item for a customer with a **leasing** or **hire purchase** arrangement. (See Unit 24) Another possibility is for the bank to lend money without interest but to cover its expenses with a **service charge**.

If a business suddenly needs very short-term capital or **working capital** for unexpected purchases and expenses, it can be difficult to get it under the PLS system. On the other hand, PLS means that **bank–customer relations** are very close, and that banks have to be very careful in evaluating projects, as they are buying shares in the company.

Conventional banks
- Pay interest to depositors
- Charge interest to borrowers
- Lend money to finance personal consumption goods

Islamic banks
- Give no return on current accounts; share profits with holders of savings accounts and investment accounts
- Share borrowers' profits (or losses)
- Buy items for personal customers with a leasing or hire-purchase arrangement

26.1 Match the two parts of the sentences. Look at A opposite to help you.

1 The basic feature of Islamic banking
2 Instead of charging and paying interest
3 Depositors in Islamic banks
4 Businesses that borrow from Islamic banks
5 Islamic banks operate in a similar way

a do not receive a fixed return.
b have to share their profits with the bank.
c Islamic banks and their customers share profits and losses.
d is that it is interest-free.
e to venture capitalists who buy companies' stocks or shares.

26.2 Which of the following statements could be made by customers of Islamic banks and which by customers of conventional banks? Look at B opposite to help you.

1 I get 1.5% on my current account and 3% on my savings account.

2 I get a variable rate of return on my savings account, depending on the bank's profitability.

3 If I open a five-year investment account, I won't be able to withdraw my money during this period, but I will receive a share of the bank's profits.

4 They offered me an overdraft of up to one month's salary.

5 If the bank makes a loss I could lose part of my savings.

26.3 Make word combinations using a word from each box. Then use the word combinations to complete the sentences below. Look at A, B and C opposite to help you.

investment service risk working	capitalists capital charge account

1 All businesses need .... for everyday purchases and expenses.
2 I don't pay interest but the bank adds a .... to cover its expenses.
3 Islamic banks are like the .... who buy the shares of new companies.
4 The bank pays me some of its profits on the money I have in my ....

Over to you

What do you think are the advantages and disadvantages of profit and loss sharing compared with charging interest?

27 Money supply and control

A Measuring money

Professor John Webb, the banking expert we met in Unit 23, continues his interview.

What is the **money supply**?

It's the stock of money and the supply of new money. The currency **in circulation** – coins and notes that people spend – makes up only a very small part of the money supply. The rest consists of bank deposits.

Are there different ways of measuring it?

Yes. It depends on whether you include **time deposits** – bank deposits that can only be withdrawn after a certain period of time. The smallest measure is called **narrow money**. This only includes currency and **sight deposits** – bank deposits that customers can withdraw whenever they like. The other measures are of **broad money**. This includes savings deposits and time deposits, as well as money market funds, certificates of deposit, commercial paper, repurchase agreements, and things like that. (See Unit 25)

What about spending?

To measure money you also have to know how often it is spent in a given period. This is money's **velocity of circulation** – how quickly it moves from one institution or bank account to another. In other words, the quantity of money spent is the money supply times its velocity of circulation.

B Changing the money supply

The **monetary authorities** – sometimes the government, but usually the central bank – use **monetary policy** to try to control the amount of money in circulation, and its growth. This is in order to prevent inflation – the continuous increase in prices, which reduces the amount of things that people can buy.

- They can change the **discount rate** at which the central bank lends short-term funds to commercial banks. The lower interest rates are, the more money people and businesses borrow, which increases the money supply.
- They can change commercial banks' **reserve–asset ratio**. (See Unit 23) This sets the percentage of deposits a bank has to keep in its reserves (for depositors who wish to withdraw their money), which is generally around 8%. The more a bank has to keep, the less it can lend.
- The central bank can also buy or sell treasury bills in open-market operations with commercial banks. If the banks buy these bonds, they have less money (and so can lend less), and if the central bank buys them back, the commercial banks have more money to lend.

C Monetarism

Monetarist economists are those who argue that if you control the money supply, you can control **inflation**. They believe the average levels of prices and wages depend on the quantity of money in circulation and its velocity of circulation. They think that inflation is caused by too much **monetary growth**: too much new money being added to the money stock. Other economists disagree. They say the money supply can grow because of increased economic activity: more goods being sold and more services being performed.

27.1 Are the following statements true or false? Find reasons for your answers in A and B opposite.

1 Most money exists on paper, in bank accounts, rather than in notes and coins.
2 Banking customers can withdraw time deposits whenever they like.
3 The amount of money spent is the money supply multiplied by its velocity of circulation.
4 Central banks can try to control the money supply.
5 Commercial banks can choose which percentage of their deposits they keep in their reserves.

27.2 Use the words below to make word combinations with 'money'. Then use the word combinations to complete the sentences. Look at A opposite to help you.

broad	supply	narrow

1 The .... is the existing stock of money plus newly created money.
2 The smallest or most restrictive measure is ....
3 .... is a measure of money that includes savings deposits.

27.3 Find three nouns in B and C opposite that make word combinations with 'monetary'. Then use the word combinations to complete the sentences below.

monetary ....
....
....

1 The .... are the official agencies that can try to control the quantity of money.
2 The attempt to control the amount of money in circulation and the rate of inflation is called ....
3 Monetarism is the theory that the level of prices is determined by ....

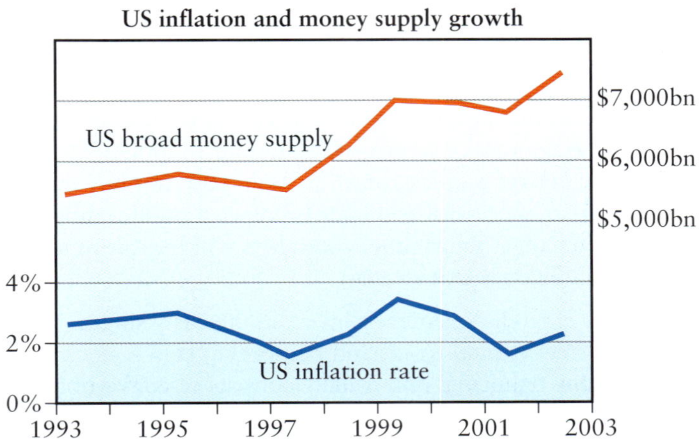

Over to you

What is wrong with having inflation? What is the current inflation rate in your country? Has this changed a lot over the past 20 years? Try to discover what factors have caused any changes.

28 Venture capital

A Raising capital

Alex Rodriguez works for a venture capital company:

'As you know, new businesses, called **start-ups**, are all **private companies** that aren't allowed to sell stocks or shares to the general public. They have to find other ways of raising capital. Some very small companies are able to operate on money their **founders** – the people who start the company – have previously saved, but larger companies need to get capital from somewhere else. As everybody knows, banks are usually **risk-averse**. This means they are unwilling to **lend** to new companies where there's a danger that they won't get their money back. But there are firms like ours that specialize in finding **venture capital**: funds for new enterprises.

Some venture capital or risk capital companies use their own funds to lend money to companies, but most of them raise capital from other financial institutions. Some rich people, who banks call **high net worth individuals**, and who we call **angels** or **angel investors**, also invest in start-ups. Although new companies present a high level of risk, they also have the potential for rapid growth – and consequently high profits – if the new business is successful. Because of this profit potential, institutions like pension funds and insurance companies are increasingly investing in new companies, particularly hi-tech ones.'

Note: **Venture capital** is also called **risk capital** or **start-up capital**.

B Return on capital

'Venture capitalists like ourselves expect **entrepreneurs** – people with an idea to start a new company – to provide us with a **business plan**. (See Unit 50)

Because of the high level of risk involved, investors in start-ups usually expect a higher than average **rate of return** – the amount of money the investment pays – on their capital. If they can't get a quick return in cash, they can buy the new company's shares. If the company is successful and later becomes a **public company**, which means it is listed on a stock exchange, the venture capitalists will be able to sell their shares then, at a profit. This will be their **exit strategy**.

Venture capitalists generally invest in the early stages of a new company. Some companies need further capital to expand before they join a stock exchange. This is often called **mezzanine financing**, and usually consists of **convertible bonds** – bonds that can later be converted to shares (see Unit 33) – or **preference shares** that receive a fixed dividend. (See Unit 29) Investors providing money at this stage have a lower risk of loss than earlier investors like us, but also less chance of making a big profit.'

BrE: preference shares; AmE: preferred stock

28.1 Complete the crossword. Look at A and B opposite to help you.

Across

3 A firm listed on a stock exchange is a .... (6,7)
7 Individuals who lend money to new companies are sometimes called .... (6)
8 Banks that are risk- .... usually don't want to finance new companies. (6)
10 The amount of money made from an investment is its rate of .... (6)
11 New businesses often have to get finance from .... companies. (4,7)
12 The people who start companies. (8)

Down

1 People who have ideas for setting up new businesses. (13)
2 .... capital firms specialise in financing new companies. (7)
4 Many banks don't want to .... money to new businesses. (4)
5 People who want to borrow money to start a company write a business .... (4)
6 Money invested in a company just before it joins a stock exchange is sometimes called .... financing. (9)
9 and 13 down A new company is often called a .... (5-2)
13 See 9 down.

28.2 Match the two parts of the sentences. Look at A and B opposite to help you.

1 Banks are usually reluctant
2 Start-ups often get money
3 New companies can grow rapidly
4 Risk capitalists usually expect
5 Venture capitalists need an exit strategy – a way
6 Mezzanine financing is a second round of financing

a a higher than average return on their money.
b and so are potentially profitable.
c before a company joins a stock exchange.
d to get their money back after a few years.
e to lend money to new companies.
f from specialized venture capital firms.

Over to you

Would you invest in start-ups? In which fields? If you wanted to start a business, how would you try to raise capital?

29 Stocks and shares 1

A Stocks, shares and equities

Stocks and **shares** are certificates representing part ownership of a company. The people who own them are called **stockholders** and **shareholders.** In Britain, stock is also used to refer to all kinds of securities, including government bonds. (See Unit 33) The word **equity** or **equities** is also used to describe stocks and shares. The places where the stocks and shares of **listed** or **quoted** companies are bought and sold are called **stock markets** or **stock exchanges.**

B Going public

A successful existing company wants to expand, and decides to **go public.**

↓

The company gets advice from an investment bank about how many shares to offer and at what price.

↓

The company gets independent accountants to produce a **due diligence** report.

↓

The company produces a **prospectus** which explains its financial position, and gives details about the senior managers and the **financial results** from previous years.

↓

The company makes a **flotation** or **IPO** (**initial public offering**).

↓

An investment bank **underwrites** the stock issue.

go public: change from a private company to a public limited company (PLC) by selling shares to outside investors for the first time (with a flotation)

due diligence: a detailed examination of a company and its financial situation

prospectus: a document inviting the public to buy shares, stating the terms of sale and giving information about the company

financial results: details about sales, costs, debts, profits, losses, etc. (See Units 11–14)

flotation: an offer of a company's shares to investors (financial institutions and the general public)

underwrites a stock issue: guarantees to buy the shares if there are not enough other buyers

Note: **Flotation** can also be spelt **floatation**.

BrE: ordinary shares; AmE: common stock

C Ordinary and preference shares

If a company has only one type of share these are **ordinary shares.** Some companies also have **preference shares** whose holders receive a **fixed dividend** (e.g. 5% of the shares' nominal value) that must be paid before holders of ordinary shares receive a dividend. Holders of preference shares have more chance of getting some of their capital back if a company **goes bankrupt** – stops trading because it is unable to pay its debts. If the company **goes into liquidation** – has to sell all its assets to repay part of its debts – holders of preference shares are repaid before other shareholders, but after owners of bonds and other debts. If shareholders expect a company to grow, however, they generally prefer ordinary shares to preference shares, because the dividend is likely to increase over time.

29.1 Match the words in the box with the definitions below. Look at A, B and C opposite to help you.

bankrupt	prospectus
going public	ordinary shares
flotation	preference shares
investors	stock exchange
liquidation	to underwrite

1 a document describing a company and offering stocks for sale
2 a market on which companies' stocks are traded
3 buyers of stocks
4 changing from a private company to a public one, quoted on a stock exchange
5 the first sale of a company's stocks to the public
6 to guarantee to buy newly issued shares if no one else does
7 shares that pay a guaranteed dividend
8 the most common form of shares
9 insolvent, unable to pay debts
10 the sale of the assets of a failed company

29.2 Are the following statements true or false? Find reasons for your answers in A, B and C opposite.

1 New companies can apply to join a stock exchange.
2 Investment banks sometimes have to buy some of the stocks in an IPO.
3 The due diligence report is produced by the company's own accountants.
4 The dividend paid on preference shares is variable.
5 If a company goes bankrupt, the first investors to get any money back are the holders of preference shares.

29.3 Make word combinations using a word or phrase from each box. Then use the correct forms of the word combinations to complete the sentences below. Look at A, B and C opposite to help you.

offer	an issue
go	a prospectus
produce	shares
underwrite	public

After three very profitable years, the company is planning to (1) .... (2) .... and we're (3) .... 100,000 (4) .... for sale. We've (5) .... a very attractive (6) .... , and although a leading investment bank is (7) .... the (8) .... , we don't think they'll have to buy any of the shares.

Over to you

Have there been any big flotations in the news recently? Are there any private companies whose stocks you would like to buy if they went public?

30 Stocks and shares 2

A Buying and selling shares

After newly issued shares have been sold (usually by investment banks) for the first time – this is called the **primary market** – they can be repeatedly traded at the stock exchange on which the company is listed, on what is called the **secondary market**.

Major stock exchanges, such as New York and London, have a lot of requirements about publishing financial information for shareholders. Most companies use **over-the-counter** (**OTC**) markets, such as NASDAQ in New York and the Alternative Investment Market (AIM) in London, which have fewer regulations.

The **nominal value** of a share – the price written on it – is rarely the same as its **market price** – the price it is currently being traded at on the stock exchange. This can change every minute during trading hours, because it depends on **supply** and **demand** – how many sellers and buyers there are. Some stock exchanges have computerized **automatic trading systems** that match up buyers and sellers. Other markets have **market makers:** traders in stocks who quote **bid** (buying) and **offer** (selling) prices. The **spread** or difference between these prices is their profit or **mark-up.** Most customers **place** their buying and selling **orders** with a **stockbroker:** someone who trades with the market makers.

B New share issues

Companies that require further capital can issue new shares. If these are offered to existing shareholders first this is known as a **rights issue** – because the current shareholders have the first right to buy them. Companies can also choose to **capitalize** part of their profit or retained earnings. This means turning their profits into capital by issuing new shares to existing shareholders instead of paying them a dividend. There are various names for this process, including **scrip issue**, **capitalization issue** and **bonus issue.** Companies with surplus cash can also choose to buy back some of their shares on the secondary market. These are then called **own shares.**

BrE: own shares;
AmE: treasury stock

C Categories of stocks and shares

Investors tend to classify the stocks and shares available in the **equity markets** in different categories.

- **Blue chips:** Stocks in large companies with a reputation for quality, reliability and profitability. More than two-thirds of all blue chips in industrialized countries are owned by institutional investors such as insurance companies and pension funds.
- **Growth stocks:** Stocks that are expected to regularly rise in value. Most technology companies are growth stocks, and don't pay dividends, so the shareholders' equity or owners' equity increases. This causes the stock price to rise. (See Unit 11)
- **Income stocks:** Stocks that have a history of paying consistently high dividends.
- **Defensive stocks:** Stocks that provide a regular dividend and stable earnings, but whose value is not expected to rise or fall very much.
- **Value stocks:** Stocks that investors believe are currently trading for less than they are worth – when compared with the companies' assets.

30.1 Match the words in the box with the definitions below. Look at A and B opposite to help you.

to capitalize	market price	primary market	own shares
rights issue	secondary market	nominal value	

1 new shares offered to existing shareholders
2 the price written on a share, which never changes
3 to turn profits into stocks or shares
4 the market on which shares can be re-sold
5 the price at which a share is currently being traded
6 shares that companies have bought back from their owners
7 the market on which new shares are sold

30.2 Are the following statements true or false? Find reasons for your answers in A and B opposite.

1 Stocks that have already been bought at least once are traded on the primary market.
2 NASDAQ and the AIM have more regulations than the New York Stock Exchange and the London Stock Exchange.
3 The market price of stocks depends on how many buyers and sellers there are.
4 Automatic trading systems do not require market makers.
5 Market makers make a profit from the difference between their bid and offer prices.

30.3 Complete the sentences. Look at B and C opposite to help you.

1 A stock whose price has suddenly fallen a lot after a company had bad news could be a .... , as it will probably rise again.

2 The stocks of food, tobacco and oil companies are usually .... , as demand doesn't rise or fall very much in periods of economic expansion or contraction.

3 Pension funds and insurance companies, which can't take risks, usually only invest in ....

4 The best way to make a profit in the long term is to invest in ....

5 This stock used to be considered an .... , but two years ago the company started to cut its dividend and reinvest its cash in the business.

6 The financial director announced a forthcoming .... of new shares to existing shareholders.

7 The company is planning a .... of one additional share for every three existing shares.

8 We have bought back 200,000 ordinary shares, which increases the value of our .... to €723,000.

Over to you

If you had a lot of money to invest in stocks, what kind of stocks would you buy, and why?

31 Shareholders

A Investors

Stock markets are measured by **stock indexes** (or indices), such as the Dow Jones Industrial Average (DJIA) in New York, and the FTSE 100 index (often called the Footsie) in London. These indexes show changes in the average prices of a selected group of important stocks. There have been several stock market **crashes** when these indexes have fallen considerably on a single day (e.g. 'Black Monday', 19 October 1987, when the DJIA lost 22.6%).

Financial journalists use some animal names to describe investors:

- **bulls** are investors who expect prices to rise
- **bears** are investors who expect them to fall
- **stags** are investors who buy new share issues hoping that they will be **over-subscribed.** This means they hope there will be more demand than available stocks, so the successful buyers can immediately sell their stocks at a profit.

A period when most of the stocks on a market rise is called a **bull market.** A period when most of them fall in value is a **bear market.**

B Dividends and capital gains

Companies that **make a profit** either **pay a dividend** to their stockholders, or **retain** their **earnings** by keeping the profits in the company, which causes the value of the stocks to rise. Stockholders can then make a **capital gain** – increase the amount of money they have – by selling their stocks at a higher price than they paid for them. Some stockholders prefer not to receive dividends, because the tax they pay on capital gains is lower than the income tax they pay on dividends. When an investor buys shares on the secondary market they are either **cum div**, meaning the investor will receive the next dividend the company pays, or **ex div**, meaning they will not. Cum div share prices are higher, as they include the estimated value of the coming dividend.

C Speculators

Institutional investors generally keep stocks for a long period, but there are also **speculators** – people who buy and sell shares rapidly, hoping to make a profit. These include **day traders** – people who buy stocks and sell them again before the **settlement day.** This is the day on which they have to pay for the stocks they have purchased, usually three business days after the trade was made. If day traders sell at a profit before settlement day, they never have to pay for their shares. Day traders usually work with **online brokers** on the internet, who charge low **commissions** – fees for buying or selling stocks for customers. Speculators who expect a price to fall can **take a short position,** which means agreeing to sell stocks in the future at their current price, before they actually own them. They then wait for the price to fall before buying and selling the stocks. The opposite – a **long position** – means actually **owning a security** or other asset: that is buying it and having it recorded in one's account.

June 1: Sell 1,000 Microsoft stocks, to be delivered June 4, at current market price: $26.20

June 3: Stock falls to $25.90. Buy 1,000

June 4: Settlement day. Pay for 1,000 stocks @ $25.90, receive 1,000 x $26.20. Profit $300

A short position

31.1 Label the graph with words from the box. Look at A opposite to help you.

bull market	crash	bear market

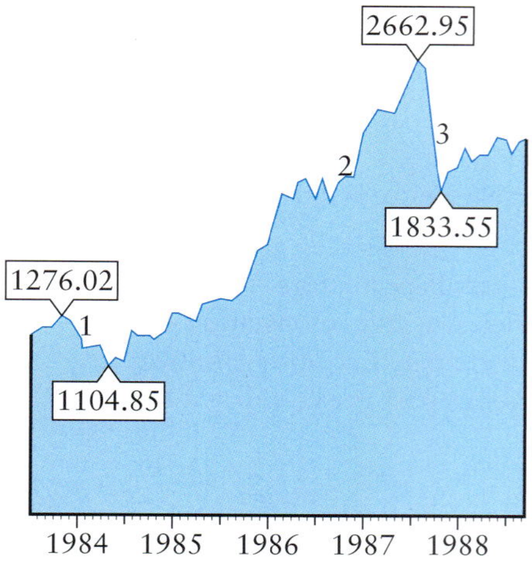

1 ....
2 ....
3 ....

31.2 Answer the questions. Look at A, B and C opposite to help you.

1 How do stags make a profit?
2 Why do some investors prefer not to receive dividends?
3 How do you make a profit from a short position?

31.3 Make word combinations using a word or phrase from each box. Some words can be used twice. Then use the correct forms of the word combinations to complete the sentences below. Look at B and C opposite to help you.

make own pay receive retain take	a capital gain a dividend earnings a position a profit securities tax

1 I .... less .... on capital gains than on income. So as a shareholder, I prefer not to .... a .... If the company .... its .... , I can .... a .... by selling my shares at a profit instead.
2 Day trading is exciting because if a share price falls, you can .... a .... by .... a short .... But it's risky selling .... that you don't even ....

The sculpture of a bull near the New York Stock Exchange

Over to you

Would you like to be a day trader? Or would you be frightened of taking such risks?

32 Share prices

A Influences on share prices

Share prices depend on a number of factors:

- the financial situation of the company
- the situation of the industry in which the company operates
- the state of the economy in general
- the beliefs of investors – whether they believe the share price will rise or fall, and whether they believe other investors will think this.

Prices can go up or down and the question for investors – and speculators – is: can these price changes be **predicted**, or seen in advance? When **price-sensitive information** – news that affects a company's value – arrives, a share price will change. But no one knows when or what that information will be. So information about past prices will not tell you what tomorrow's price will be.

B Predicting prices

There are different theories about whether share price changes can be predicted.

- The **random walk hypothesis**. Prices move along a 'random walk' – this means day-to-day changes are completely **random** or unpredictable.
- The **efficient market hypothesis**. Share prices always **accurately** or exactly reflect all relevant information. It is therefore a waste of time to attempt to discover **patterns** or **trends** – general changes in behaviour – in price movements.

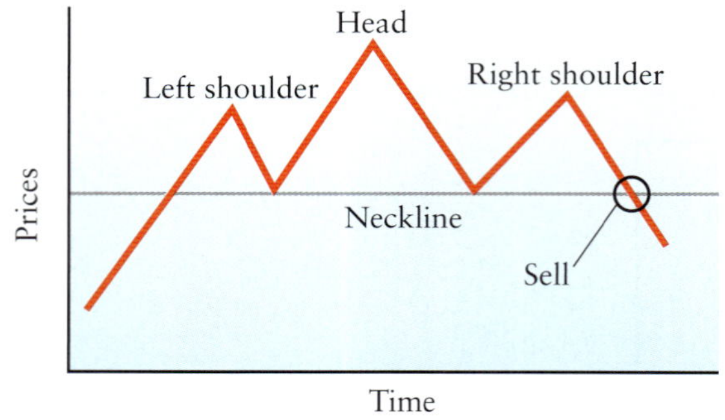

Head and shoulders pattern

- **Technical analysis**. Technical **analysts** are people who believe that studying past share prices does allow them to forecast future price changes. They believe that market prices result from the psychology of investors rather than from real economic values, so they look for trends in buying and selling behaviour, such as the 'head and shoulders' pattern.
- **Fundamental analysis**. This is the opposite of technical analysis: it ignores the behaviour of investors and assumes that a share has a true or correct value, which might be different from its stock market value. This means that markets are not efficient. The true value reflects the present value of the future income from dividends.

C Types of risk

Analysts distinguish between **systematic risk** and **unsystematic risk**. Unsystematic risks are things that affect individual companies, such as production problems or a sudden fall in sales. Investors can reduce these by having a **diversified portfolio**: buying lots of different types of securities. Systematic risks, however, cannot be eliminated in this way. For example **market risk** cannot be avoided by **diversification**: if a stock market falls, all the shares listed on it will fall to some extent.

32.1 Match the two parts of the sentences. Look at A and B opposite to help you.

1 The random walk theory states that
2 The efficient market hypothesis is that
3 Technical analysts believe that
4 Fundamental analysts believe that

a studying charts of past stock prices allows you to predict future changes.
b stocks are correctly priced so it is impossible to make a profit by finding undervalued ones.
c you can calculate a stock's true value, which might not be the same as its market price.
d it is impossible to predict future changes in stock prices.

32.2 Are the following statements true or false? Find reasons for your answers in B and C opposite.

1 Fundamental analysts think that stock prices depend on psychological factors – what people think and feel – rather than pure economic data.
2 Fundamental analysts say that the true value of a stock is all the income it will bring an investor in the future, measured at today's money values.
3 Investors can protect themselves against unknown, unsystematic risks by having a broad collection of different investments.
4 Unsystematic risks can affect an investor's entire portfolio.

32.3 Match the theories (1–3) to the statements (a–c). Look at B opposite to help you.

1 fundamental analysis
2 technical analysis
3 efficient market hypothesis

a Share prices are correct at any given time. When new information appears, they change to a new correct price.

b By analysing a company, you can determine its real value. This sometimes allows you to make a profit by buying underpriced shares.

c It's not only the facts about a company that matter: the stock price also depends on what investors think or feel about the company's future.

Over to you

Do you believe that it is possible to find undervalued stocks, predict future price changes, and regularly get returns that are higher than the stock market average?

33 Bonds

A Government and corporate bonds

Bonds are loans to local and national governments and to large companies. The holders of bonds generally receive **fixed interest payments**, once or twice a year, and get their money – known as the **principal** – back on a given **maturity date**. This is the date when the loan ends.

Governments issue bonds to raise money and they are considered to be a risk-free investment. In Britain **government bonds** are known as **gilt-edged stock** or just **gilts**. In the US they are called **Treasury notes**, which have a maturity of 2–10 years, and **Treasury bonds**, which have a maturity of 10–30 years. (There are also short-term Treasury bills which have a different function: see Units 25 and 27.)

Companies issue bonds, called **corporate bonds**, because they can usually pay less interest to bondholders than they would have to pay if they raised the same money by a bank loan. These bonds are generally safer than shares, because if a company cannot repay its debts it can be declared bankrupt. If this happens, the creditors can force the company to stop doing business, and sell its assets to repay them. In this way, bondholders will probably get some of their money back.

Borrowers – the companies issuing bonds – are given **credit ratings** by credit agencies such as Standard & Poor's and Moody's. This means that they are graded, or rated, according to their ability to repay the loan to the bondholders. The highest grade (AAA or Aaa) means that there is almost no risk that the borrower will **default** – fail to pay interest or to repay the principal. Lower grades (e.g. Baa, BBB, C, etc.) mean an increasing risk of the borrower becoming **insolvent** – unable to pay interest or repay the capital.

B Prices and yields

Bonds are traded by banks which act as market makers for their customers, quoting bid and offer prices with a very small spread or difference between them. (See Unit 30) The price of bonds varies **inversely** with interest rates. This means that if interest rates rise, so that new borrowers have to pay a higher rate, existing bonds lose value. If interest rates fall, existing bonds paying a higher interest rate than the market rate increase in value. Consequently the **yield** of a bond – how much income it gives – depends on its purchase price as well as its **coupon** or interest rate. There are also **floating-rate notes** – bonds whose interest rate varies with market interest rates.

C Other types of bonds

When interest rates are high, some companies issue **convertible shares** or **convertibles**, which are bonds that the owner can later change into shares. Convertibles pay lower interest rates than ordinary bonds, because the buyer gets the chance of making a profit with the convertible option.

There are also **zero coupon bonds** that pay no interest but are sold at a big discount on their par value, which is 100%, and repaid at 100% at maturity. Because they pay no interest, their owners don't receive money every year (and so don't have to decide how to reinvest it); instead they make a **capital gain** at maturity.

Bonds with a low credit rating (and a high chance of default), but paying a high interest rate, are called **junk bonds**. Some of these are known as **fallen angels** – bonds of companies that were previously in a good financial situation, while others are issued to finance leveraged buyouts. (See Unit 40)

BrE: convertible share; AmE: convertible bond

33.1 Match the words in the box with the definitions below. Look at A and B opposite to help you.

coupon	maturity date
credit rating	principal
gilt-edged stock	Treasury bonds
default	Treasury notes
insolvent	yield

1 the amount of capital making up a loan
2 an estimation of a borrower's solvency or ability to pay debts
3 bonds issued by the British government
4 non-payment of interest or a loan at the scheduled time
5 the day when a bond has to be repaid
6 long-term bonds issued by the American government
7 the amount of interest that a bond pays
8 medium-term (2–10 year) bonds issued by the American government
9 the rate of income an investor receives from a security
10 unable to pay debts

33.2 Are the following statements true or false? Find reasons for your answers in A, B and C opposite.

1 Bonds are repaid at 100% when they mature, unless the borrower is insolvent.
2 Bondholders are guaranteed to get all their money back if a company goes bankrupt.
3 AAA bonds are a very safe investment.
4 A bond paying 5% interest would gain in value if interest rates rose to 6%.
5 The price of floating-rate notes doesn't vary very much, because they always pay market interest rates.
6 The owners of convertibles have to change them into shares.
7 Some bonds do not pay interest, but are repaid at above their selling price.
8 Junk bonds have a high credit rating, and a relatively low chance of default.

33.3 Answer the questions. Look at A, B and C opposite to help you.

1 Which is the safest for an investor?
A a corporate bond B a junk bond C a government bond
2 Which is the cheapest way for a company to raise money?
A a bank loan B an ordinary bond C a convertible
3 Which gives the highest potential return to an investor?
A a corporate bond B a junk bond C a government bond
4 Which is the most profitable for an investor if interest rates rise?
A a Treasury bond B a floating-rate note C a Treasury note

Over to you

Is this a good time to buy bonds? Why/why not?

34 Futures

A Commodity futures

Forward and **futures contracts** are agreements to sell an asset at a fixed price on a fixed date in the future. **Futures** are traded on a wide range of agricultural products (including wheat, maize, soybeans, pork, beef, sugar, tea, coffee, cocoa and orange juice), industrial metals (aluminium, copper, lead, nickel and zinc), precious metals (gold, silver, platinum and palladium) and oil. These products are known as **commodities**. Futures were invented to enable regular buyers and sellers of commodities to protect themselves against losses or to **hedge** against future changes in the price. If they both agree to hedge, the seller (e.g. an orange grower) is protected from a fall in price and the buyer (e.g. an orange juice manufacturer) is protected from a rise in price.

Futures are **standardized** contracts – contracts which are for fixed quantities (such as one ton of copper or 100 ounces of gold) and fixed time periods (normally three, six or nine months) – that are traded on a special exchange. **Forwards** are individual, **non-standardized** contracts between two parties, traded **over-the-counter** – directly, between two companies or financial institutions, rather than through an exchange. The futures price for a commodity is normally higher than its **spot price** – the price that would be paid for immediate delivery. Sometimes, however, short-term demand pushes the spot price above the future price. This is called **backwardation**.

Futures and forwards are also used by speculators – people who hope to profit from price changes.

BrE: aluminium; AmE: aluminum

B Financial futures

More recently, **financial futures** have been developed. These are standardized contracts, traded on exchanges, to buy and sell financial assets. Financial assets such as currencies, interest rates, stocks and stock market indexes **fluctuate** – continuously vary – so financial futures are used to fix a value for a specified future date (e.g. sell euros for dollars at a rate of €1 for $1.20 on June 30).

- **Currency futures** and **forwards** are contracts that specify the price at which a certain currency will be bought or sold on a specified date.
- **Interest rate futures** are agreements between banks and investors and companies to issue fixed income securities (bonds, certificates of deposit, money market deposits, etc.) at a future date.
- **Stock futures** fix a price for a stock and **stock index futures** fix a value for an index (e.g. the Dow Jones or the FTSE) on a certain date. They are alternatives to buying the stocks or shares themselves.

Like futures for physical commodities, financial futures can be used both to hedge and to speculate. Obviously the buyer and seller of a financial future have different opinions about what will happen to exchange rates, interest rates and stock prices. They are both taking an unlimited risk, because there could be huge changes in rates and prices during the period of the contract. Futures trading is a **zero-sum game**, because the amount of money gained by one party will be the same as the sum lost by the other.

34.1 Match the words in the box with the definitions below. Look at A opposite to help you.

backwardation	commodities	forwards	futures
to hedge	over-the-counter	spot price	

1 the price for the immediate purchase and delivery of a commodity
2 the situation when the current price is higher than the future price
3 adjective describing a contract made between two businesses, not using an exchange
4 contracts for non-standardized quantities or time periods
5 physical substances, such as food, fuel and metals, that can be bought or sold with futures contracts
6 to protect yourself against loss
7 contracts to buy or sell standardized quantities

34.2 Complete the sentences using a word or phrase from each box. Look at A and B opposite to help you.

A Commodity futures allow
B Interest rate futures allow
C Currency futures allow

u banks	x food manufacturers
v companies	y importers
w farmers	z investors

1 .... to charge a consistent price for their products.
2 .... to be sure of the rate they will get on bonds which could be issued at a different rate in the future.
3 .... to know at what price they can borrow money to finance new projects.
4 .... to make plans knowing what price they will get for their crops.
5 .... to offer fixed lending rates.
6 .... to remove exchange rate risks from future international purchases.

34.3 Are the following statements true or false? Find reasons for your answers in B opposite.

1 Financial futures were created because exchange rates, interest rates and stock prices all regularly change.
2 Interest rate futures are related to stocks and shares.
3 Financial futures contracts allow companies to protect themselves against short-term changes in exchange rates.
4 You can only hedge if someone who expects a price to move in the opposite direction is willing to buy or sell a contract.
5 Both parties can make money out of the same futures contract.

Over to you

Look at some commodity prices, and decide if you think they will rise or fall over the next three months. Check in three months' time to see if you would have made or lost money by buying or selling futures.

35 Derivatives

A Options

Derivatives are financial products whose value depends on – or is derived from – another financial product, such as a stock, a stock market index, or interest rate payments. They can be used to manage the risks associated with securities, to protect against fluctuations in value, or to speculate. The main kinds of derivatives are **options** and **swaps**.

Options are like futures (see Unit 34) except that they **give the right** – give the possibility, but not the obligation – to buy or sell an asset in the future (e.g. 1,000 General Electric stocks on 31 March). If you **buy** a **call option** it gives you the right to buy an asset for a specific price, either at any time before the option ends or on a specific future date. However, if you **buy** a **put option**, it gives you the right to sell an asset at a specific price within a specified period or on a specific future date. Investors can buy put options to hedge against falls in the price of stocks.

B In-the-money and out-of-the-money

Selling or **writing** options contracts involves the obligation either to deliver or to buy assets, if the buyer **exercises the option** – chooses to make the trade. For this the seller (writer) receives a fee called a **premium** from the buyer. But writers of options do not expect them to be exercised. For example, if you expect the price of a stock to rise from 100 to 120, you can buy a call option giving the right to buy the stock at 110. If the stock price does not rise to 110, you will not exercise the option, and the seller of the option will gain the premium. Your option will be **out-of-the-money**, as the stock is trading at below the **strike price** or **exercise price** of 110, the price stated in the option. If, on the other hand, the stock price rises above 110, you are **in-the-money**: you can exercise the option and you will gain the difference between the current market price and 110. If the market moves in an unexpected direction, the writers of options can lose enormous amounts of money.

C Warrants and swaps

Some companies issue **warrants** which, like options, give the right, but not the obligation, to buy stocks in the future at a particular price, probably higher than the current market price. They are usually issued along with bonds, but they can generally be detached from the bonds and traded separately. Unlike call options, which last three, six or nine months, warrants have long maturities of up to ten years.

Swaps are arrangements between institutions to exchange interest rates or currencies (e.g. dollars for yen). For example, a company that has borrowed money by issuing floating-rate notes (see Unit 33) could protect itself from a rise in interest rates by arranging with a bank to swap its floating-rate payments for a fixed-rate payment, if the bank expected interest rates to fall.

35.1 Match the two parts of the sentences. Look at A opposite to help you.

1 The price of a derivative always depends on
2 Options can be used to hedge against
3 A call option gives its owner
4 A put option gives its owner

a future price changes.
b the right to buy something.
c the price of another financial product.
d the right to sell something.

35.2 Choose the correct endings for the sentences. Some sentences have more than one possible ending. Look at A and B opposite to help you.

1 If you expect the price of a stock to rise, you can
a buy a call option.
b sell a call option.
c buy a put option.
d sell a put option.

2 If you expect the price of a stock to fall, you can
a buy a call option.
b sell a call option.
c buy a put option.
d sell a put option.

3 If an option is out-of-the-money it will
a be exercised.
b not be exercised.

4 If an option is in-the-money the seller will
a lose money.
b gain money.

5 The bigger risk is taken by
a writers of options.
b buyers of options.

35.3 Complete the definitions. Look at A, B and C opposite to help you.

1 .... are like call options, but with much longer time spans.

2 .... give the right to sell securities at a fixed price within a specified period.

3 .... can be used to speculate on interest rate movements.

35.4 Complete these sentences using words from A, B and C opposite.

1 If your put option is out-of-the-money, the seller will gain the ....
2 You only exercise a call option if the market price is higher than the ....
3 If I expect a stock price to go up in the short term, I buy .... instead of the stock.
4 If I expect a big company's stock price to go up in the long term, I sometimes buy their ....
5 We needed euros and had a lot of dollars in the bank, so we did a .... with a German company which needed dollars.

Over to you

Buying and selling options and swaps is highly risky: one party in the deal is guaranteed to lose. Would you like to have a job which required you to buy and sell these products?

36 Asset management

A Allocating and diversifying assets

These are a student's notes from a lecture about asset management.

WHAT? **Asset management** is managing financial assets for institutions or individuals.
WHO? Pension funds and insurance companies manage huge amounts of money. Private banks specialize in managing **portfolios** of wealthy individuals. **Unit trusts** invest money for small investors in a range of **securities**.
HOW? Asset managers have to decide how to **allocate** funds they're responsible for: how much to invest in shares, mutual funds, bonds, cash, foreign currencies, precious metals, or other types of investments.
WHY? **Asset allocation** decisions depend on objectives and size of the portfolio (see below). The portfolio's objectives determine the returns expected or needed, and the acceptable level of risk. The best way to reduce exposure to risk is to **diversify** the portfolio – easier and cheaper for a large portfolio than a small one.

portfolio: all the investments held by an individual investor or organization

securities: a general name for shares, bonds and other tradable financial assets

allocate: to distribute according to a plan

diversify: to buy a wide variety of different securities

BrE: unit trusts; AmE: mutual funds

B Types of investor

Investors have different goals or objectives.

- Some want **regular income** from the investments – less concerned with size of their capital.
- Some want to **preserve** (keep) their capital – avoiding risks. If the goal is **capital preservation**, the asset manager usually allocates more money to bonds than stocks.
- Others want to **accumulate** or build up capital – taking more risks. If the goal is **growth** or **capital accumulation**, the portfolio will probably include more shares than bonds. Shares have better profit potential than bonds, but are also more **volatile** – their value can increase or decrease more in a short period of time.

C Active and passive investment

Some asset managers (or their clients) choose an **active strategy** – buying and selling frequently, adapting the portfolio to changing market circumstances. Others use a **passive strategy** – buying and holding securities, leaving the position unchanged for a long time.
Nowadays there are lots of **index-linked funds** which simply try to **track** or follow the movements of a stock market index. They buy lots of different stocks in the index, so if the index goes up or down, the value of the fund will too. They charge much lower **fees** than actively managed accounts – and usually do just as well. Investors in these funds believe that you can't regularly **outperform the market** – make more than average returns from the market.

BrE: index-linked fund; AmE: tracker fund

36.1 Find nouns in A and B opposite that can be used to make word combinations with the verbs below. Then use some of the word combinations to complete the sentences.

accumulate ....

diversify ....

allocate ....
....
....

manage ....
....
....
....

1 I don't want to pay a bank to .... my .... ; I can do it myself.
2 I have lots of different types of securities, because I decided to .... my ....
3 As an asset manager, I discuss clients' needs and objectives and then we decide how to .... their ....
4 If my clients want to .... , I take more risks, and buy a lot of stocks.

36.2 Match the investment goals (1–3) with the statements (a–c). Look at B opposite to help you.

1 capital preservation
2 growth
3 income

a I want to accumulate wealth, but I know that this means taking risks and buying securities with volatile prices that could go down as well as up.

b I want a regular return every year, because I need that money, even if this means I might have to risk losing some of my capital.

c I definitely don't want to risk losing any of my capital, even if this means that some years I get a very low return.

36.3 Match the two parts of the sentences. Look at A, B and C opposite to help you.

1 The value of index-linked funds will change frequently
2 Private banks
3 Asset managers buy more bonds than shares
4 Mutual funds
5 Asset managers buy more shares than bonds

a if the client wants to avoid risks.
b diversify the money of small investors.
c if the whole market is volatile.
d manage the investments of rich investors.
e if the client hopes to accumulate capital.

Over to you

What particular skills and abilities do you think an asset manager needs? Do you think you have them? Would you like to do this job?

37 Hedge funds and structured products

A Hedge funds

Hedge funds are private investment funds for wealthy investors, run by partners who have made big personal investments in the fund. They **pool** or put together their money and investors' money and trade in securities and derivatives, and try to get high returns whether markets move up or down. They are able to make big profits, but also big losses if things go wrong. Despite their name, hedge funds do not necessarily use **hedging** techniques – protecting themselves against future price changes. (See Unit 34) In fact, they generally specialize in high-risk, short-term speculation on stock options, bonds, currencies and derivatives. (See Unit 35) Because they are private, hedge funds do not have to follow as many rules as mutual funds.

B Leverage, short-selling and arbitrage

Most hedge funds use **gearing** or **leverage**, which means borrowing money as well as using their own funds, to increase the amount of capital available for investment. In this way, the fund can hold much larger **positions** or investments. Hedge funds invest where they see opportunities to make short-term profits, generally using a wide range of derivative contracts such as options and swaps. (See Unit 35) They take a **long position** by buying securities that they believe will increase in value. At the same time, they sell securities they think will decrease in value, but which they have not yet purchased. This is called taking a **short position**. If the price does fall, they can buy them at a lower price, and then sell them at a profit.

Hedge funds also use **arbitrage**, which means simultaneously purchasing a security or currency in one market and selling it, or a related derivative product, in another market, at a slightly higher price. In this way investors can profit from **price differences** between the two markets. Because the price difference is usually very small (and would be zero if markets were perfectly efficient), a huge volume is required for the **arbitrageur** to make a significant profit.

C Structured products

Investors who do not have sufficient funds to join a hedge fund can buy **structured products** from banks. These are **customized** – individualized or non-standard – over-the-counter financial instruments. They use derivative products (futures, forwards, options, warrants, etc.) in a way similar to hedge funds, depending on the customer's requirements and changes in the markets.

"The bad news is it's all our clients' money."

37.1 Match the verbs in the box with the definitions below. Look at A and B opposite to help you.

to leverage	to pool
to take a long position	to take a short position

1 to put several people's resources together for shared use
2 to purchase securities, expecting their price to rise
3 to use borrowed money as well as one's own money to increase the size of one's investments
4 to sell securities that one has not yet purchased, anticipating that their price will fall

37.2 Are the following statements true or false? Find reasons for your answers in A, B and C opposite.

1 Hedge funds are so named because they protect against losses.
2 Hedge funds use their investors' money as well as borrowed money.
3 Hedge funds concentrate on making long-term investments.
4 The fact that investors can make a profit from arbitrage shows that markets are not perfectly efficient.
5 Structured products are individualized financial instruments offered by hedge funds.

37.3 Read the advertisement for structured products from the UBS website, and answer the questions below.

The most widely used structured products can be classified into four broad categories according to their intended purpose. Derivatives are used in order to achieve the desired structures, either in combination with the underlying securities or other derivative securities.

The major groupings are:

- Capital Protection – This may be in the form of hedging, utilizing forwards, futures or swaps contracts, or it could be in the form of insurance using options.
- Yield Enhancement – This is usually achieved by writing (selling) options over an underlying asset. The premium from the written option provides the additional income yield.
- Full Participation – These are products that have similar risk characteristics as the underlying assets, but which allow the client the convenience of being able to trade unusual baskets of assets such as foreign stock indices or a specific market sector index.
- Leverage – These are generally products such as warrants, which require a low initial investment but which allow the buyer to participate in the purchase or sale of a significantly larger investment at a predetermined price in the future.

N.B. These products may carry higher risks than other classes of investment. They are not suitable and are therefore not available to every investor.

Which group of structured products would you use if:

1 you wanted the chance of big returns with only a small investment now?
2 you didn't want to lose any of your money?
3 you wanted to trade in a particular combination of assets?
4 you wanted the highest return?

Over to you

If you had a lot of money to invest, would you take the risk of joining a hedge fund? If not, why not?

38 Describing charts and graphs

A Increase and decrease

Upward movement			
Verbs		**Nouns**	
to rise	to increase	a rise	an increase
to grow	to climb	a growth	an improvement*
to improve*	to get better*	* (only for positive situations)	
*(only for positive situations)			

The basic income tax rate will rise from 25% to 28%.

ABC sales improved last year by 10% to $1m.

The UK inflation rate has climbed to 3%.

Downward movement			
Verbs		**Nouns**	
to fall	to decline	a fall	a decline
to decrease	to drop	a decrease	a drop
to deteriorate*	to get worse*	a deterioration*	
*(only for negative situations)		*(only for negative situations)	

Travel agents are expecting a 4% fall in prices.

CBA profits decreased from €4.5m to €4.2m as sales continued to deteriorate.

B Rate of change

Adjectives and adverbs can describe both the quantity and the speed of a change.

Large changes	Fast changes	Regular changes
considerable – considerably dramatic – dramatically sharp – sharply significant – significantly substantial – substantially	abrupt – abruptly quick – quickly rapid – rapidly sudden – suddenly	gradual – gradually steady – steadily
Small changes	**Slow changes**	
moderate – moderately slight – slightly	slow – slowly	

C High points, low points, and staying the same

To reach the highest point and then go down	To reach the lowest point and then rise
to peak to top out to reach a peak to reach a maximum	to hit bottom to bottom out to reach a low point
To stay at the same level on the graph or chart	**To go up and down continuously**
to remain stable to stabilize to remain constant to level off	to fluctuate

38.1 Match the graphs (1–3) to the descriptions (a–c). Look at A, B and C opposite to help you.

1

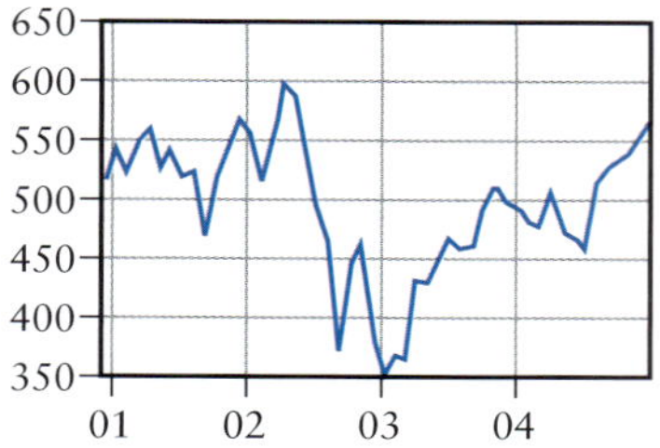

2

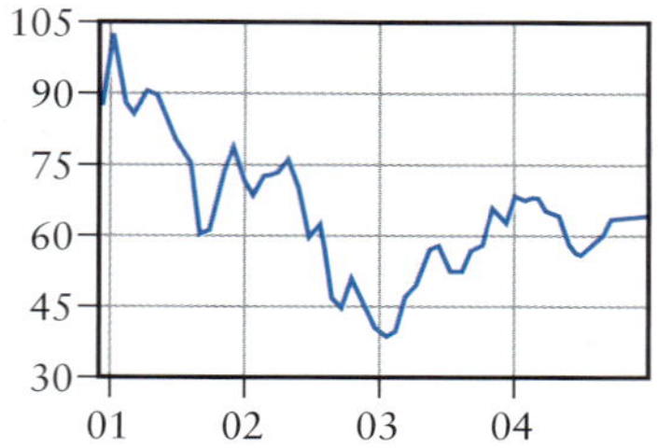

3

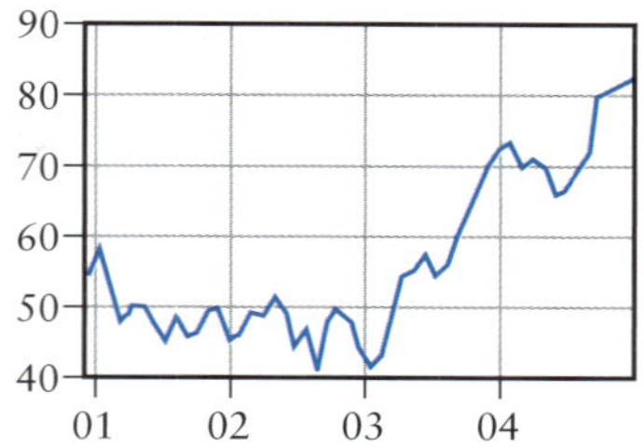

a After peaking early in 2001, Deutsche Bank shares declined for nearly two years, apart from a slight rise in the autumn of 2001. They bottomed out in early 2003, and climbed steadily for most of the year. They fell again in the summer of 2004, but the end of the year saw an improvement.

b Following a sharp fall early in 2001, UBS shares were up and down for a couple of years, reaching a low of CHF40 in September 2002. They improved steadily in 2003 and after a moderate drop in the middle of 2004 they began to increase again.

c Barclays shares reached a peak in spring 2002, and then fell steadily for six months, before rising slightly and then dropping again until the end of the year. However, 2003, saw an almost uninterrupted growth, which despite a couple of moderate falls continued in 2004.

38.2 Complete the text describing the graph with words from the box. Look at A, B and C opposite to help you.

grew slowly	increased rapidly
remained stable	risen regularly
sharp increases	

The number of hedge funds (1) .... in 1991–92 but has (2) .... ever since. Although the number of funds (3) .... between 1992 and 1997 the assets of the funds only (4) .... There were (5) .... in hedge funds' total assets in 1999 and 2003.

Growth of hedge funds

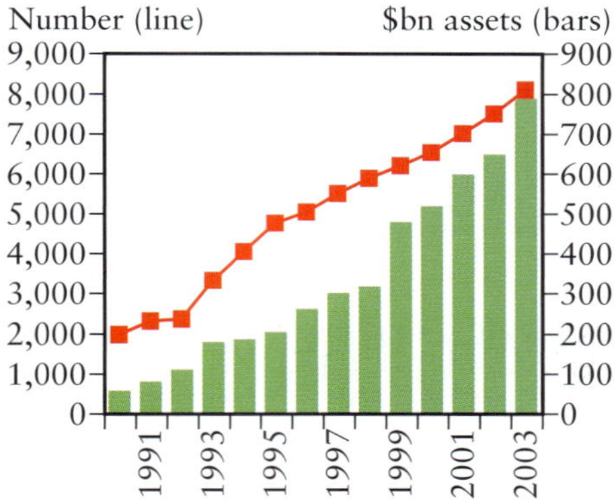

38.3 Describe the graph showing the price of gold. Look at A, B and C opposite to help you.

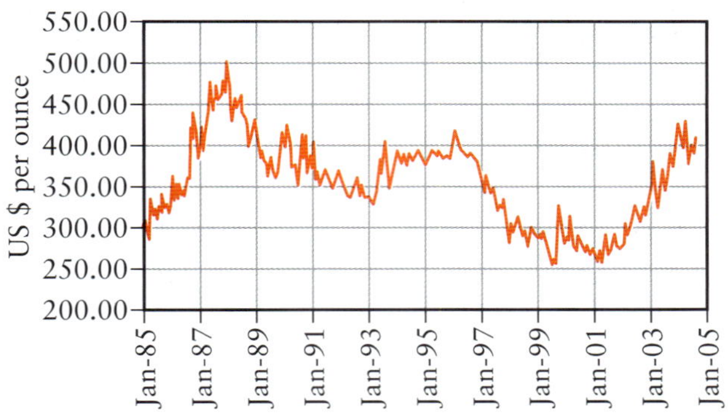

Over to you

Find a graph on the internet showing recent changes in the sales, profits or stock price of a company you are interested in, and describe it using words from the opposite page.

39 Mergers and takeovers

A Mergers, takeovers and joint ventures

In the modern business world, the ownership of companies often changes. This can happen in different ways:

- a **merger**: this is when two companies join together to form a new one (e.g. Exxon and Mobil, America Online and Time Warner).
- a **takeover** or **acquisition**: this is when one company buys another one (e.g. Vodafone and Mannesmann, Daimler-Benz and Chrysler). This can happen in two ways. Firstly, a company can offer to buy all the shareholders' shares at a certain price (higher than the market price) during a limited period of time. This is called a **takeover bid**. Secondly, a company can buy as many shares as possible on the stock market, hoping to gain a majority. This is called a **raid**.

Investment banks have **mergers and acquisitions (M&A) departments** that advise companies involved in mergers and takeovers.

Companies can also work together without a change of ownership. For example, when two or more companies decide to work together for a specific project or product, this is called a **joint venture**. An example is Sony Ericsson, which makes mobile phones.

"Well the merger is over, now the takeover starts."

B Hostile or friendly?

There are two types of takeover bid. If a company's board of directors agrees to a takeover, it is a **friendly bid** (and if the shareholders agree to sell, it becomes a **friendly takeover**). If the company does not want to be taken over, it is a **hostile bid** (and if successful, a **hostile takeover**). Companies have various ways of defending themselves against a hostile bid. They can try to find a **white knight** – another company that they would prefer to be bought by. Or they can use the **poison pill** defence ('eat me and you'll die!') which involves issuing new shares at a big discount. This reduces the holding of the company attempting the takeover, and makes the takeover much more expensive.

C Integration

Horizontal integration is when a company gets bigger by acquiring competitors in the same field of activity. **Vertical integration** is acquiring companies involved in other parts of the supply chain, usually to make cost savings. There are two possibilities: **backward integration** is acquiring suppliers of raw materials or components; **forward integration** is buying distributors or retail outlets. Companies can also buy businesses in completely different fields, which is known as **diversification**. This can be done to reduce the risk involved in operating in only one industry – but diversifying into completely different industries is a risk itself.

39.1 Complete the sentences. Look at A opposite to help you.

1 I want to work in the mergers and .... department of an investment bank in New York.
2 Beverage Partners Worldwide is a .... between the Coca-Cola and Nestlé companies, making ready-to-drink teas and coffees.
3 After their .... , Union Bank of Switzerland and Swiss Bank Corporation had combined assets of $600bn.
4 We started with a .... , buying all the stocks available on the stock exchange. That got us 15% of their stocks. Then we made a .... , offering 20% above the market price, and bought another 40% of the company.

39.2 Complete the sentences. Look at B opposite to help you.

1 Telecom Italia is looking for a .... to rescue it from a .... takeover by rival Olivetti.

2 Colonial has agreed to a .... takeover by Commonwealth Bank.

3 Mackenzie Financial Corp is planning a huge rights issue as a .... to fight off C. I. Fund Management's takeover offer.

39.3 Match the newspaper headlines (1–5) with the processes (a–e). Look at C opposite to help you.

1 **Shell Purchases 30 Gas Stations**

2 **Hotel Chain to Buy Furniture Manufacturer to Supply Its New Hotels**

3 **Electrical Retailer Dixons Bids for High Street Competitor Currys**

4 ***Coca-Cola Acquires Columbia Pictures for $700 Million***

5 **BP Now Controls the Entire Supply Chain, From the Oil Refinery to the Petrol Pump**

a horizontal integration
b vertical integration
c forward integration
d backward integration
e diversification

Over to you

Look at some financial newspapers or websites. What kind of takeover bids are taking place in your country?

40 Leveraged buyouts

A Conglomerates

A series of takeovers can result in a **parent company** controlling a number of **subsidiaries:** smaller companies that it owns. When the subsidiaries operate in many different business areas, the company is known as a **conglomerate.**

But large conglomerates can become inefficient. Top executives often leave after hostile takeovers, and too much diversification means the company is no longer concentrating on its **core business:** its central and most important activity. Takeovers do not always result in **synergy:** combined production or productivity that is greater than the sum of the separate parts. In fact, statistics show that most mergers and acquisitions reduce rather than increase a company's value.

An inefficient conglomerate whose profits are too low can have a low stock price, and its **market capitalization** – the total market price of all its ordinary shares – can fall below the value of its assets, including land, buildings and pension funds. If this happens, it becomes profitable for another company to buy the conglomerate and either split it up and sell it as individual companies, or close the companies and sell the assets. This practice, common in the USA but rare in Europe or Asia, is called **asset-stripping.** It shows that stock markets are not always efficient (see Unit 30), and that companies can sometimes be **undervalued** or **underpriced:** the price of their shares on the stock market can be too low. Some people argue that asset-stripping is a good way of using capital more efficiently; others argue that it is an unfortunate activity that destroys companies and jobs.

B Raiders

If **corporate raiders** – individuals or companies that want to take over other companies – borrow money to do so, usually by issuing bonds, the takeover is called a **leveraged buyout** or **LBO. Leveraged** means largely financed by borrowed capital. After the takeover, the raider sells subsidiaries of the company in order to pay back the bondholders.

Bonds issued to pay for takeovers are usually called **junk bonds** because they are risky: it may not be possible to sell the subsidiaries at a profit. But, because of the risk, these bonds pay a high interest rate, so some investors are happy to buy them.

Sometimes a company's own managers want to buy the company, and re-organize it. This is a **management buyout** or **MBO.** If the buyout is financed by issuing preference shares and convertibles, this is called **mezzanine financing** as it is, in a sense, halfway between debt and equity. (See Unit 28 for another use of 'mezzanine financing'.)

40.1 Match the words in the box with the definitions below. Look at A and B opposite to help you.

asset-stripping	core business	leveraged	market capitalization
parent company	subsidiaries	synergy	

1 a company that owns or controls one or more other companies
2 the main activity of a company
3 buying a company in order to sell some of its assets
4 companies partly or wholly owned by another company
5 having a lot of borrowed money compared to one's own funds
6 the total value of a company on the stock exchange
7 two things working together that produce an effect greater than the sum of their individual effects

40.2 Match the two parts of the sentences. Look at A and B opposite to help you.

1 Large conglomerates formed by takeovers
2 If a conglomerate diversifies and doesn't concentrate on its core business,
3 An inefficient conglomerate's stock market value
4 If a company is worth less than its assets,
5 Raiders do not need to have very much money of their own if

a can be less than the sale value of all its assets.
b can become inefficient, especially if they are very diversified.
c they use leverage, and issue junk bonds.
d there might not be synergies among all its different activities.
e you can make a profit by buying it and selling the parts.

40.3 Put the sequence of events in the correct order. The first stage is a. Look at B opposite to help you.

a Corporate raiders calculate that a large company is undervalued.
b Investors buy the bonds because they pay a high interest rate.
c The new owners sell some of the company's subsidiaries.
d The new owners repay the bondholders.
e The raiders buy the company.
f The raiders issue bonds to raise capital to buy the company.

1	a	2		3		4		5		6	

Over to you

What are the most diversified conglomerates you know of? Are they successful? Why do you think this is?

41 Financial planning

A Financing new investments

Alía Rahal works in the financial planning department of a large manufacturing company:

'**Financial planning** involves calculating whether new projects would be profitable. We have to calculate the probable **rate of return**: the amount of income we'd receive each year from the investment, expressed as a percentage of the total amount invested. If we're going to finance a project with our own money, the rate of return must be at least as high as we could get by depositing the money in a bank instead, or by making another risk-free investment, like buying government bonds.

If we need to borrow money to finance a new investment, its projected rate of return has to be higher than the **cost of capital** – the amount we have to pay to borrow the money.'

B Discounted cash flows

'We usually calculate the **discounted cash flow** value of an investment. This means **discounting** or reducing future cash flows to get their present values – in other words, calculating the present value of money to be received in the future. This is because the value of money decreases over time. Firstly, there's nearly always inflation, so cash will have lower **purchasing power** in the future: you'll be able to buy less with the same amount of money. And secondly, if you had the money now, you could get income by using or investing it. The return we could get by investing the money in other ways is the **opportunity cost** of capital. So waiting for money is also a cost. This is the **time value of money**: how much more it is worth to receive money now rather than in the future.'

C Comparing investment returns

'If we have to choose among possible investments in new projects, we work out the **net present value** (**NPV**) of each project by adding up all the expected cash flows, discounted to their present value, minus the initial investment. To do this, we have to select a **discount rate** or **capitalization rate**. This is usually the interest rate we pay for borrowing the capital, but we could increase it if there's a lot of uncertainty or risk.

Discounting sounds complicated, but it isn't. It's the opposite of compounding interest. For example, if you invest $1,000 at 10% for five years, it will yield 1.61 times its original value. So you get back $1,610, including $610 compound interest. A discount rate of 10% has a **discount factor** of one divided by 1.61, which is 0.62. So $620 invested now will be worth $1,000 in five years if it's invested at 10%.

When we're comparing alternative investments, we also calculate the **internal rate of return** (**IRR**). That's the interest rate or discount rate that gives a net present value of zero in today's money values. In other words, the present value of the cash that we're going to receive from an investment is the same as the present value of borrowing that cash. We normally choose the investment with the highest IRR.'

41.1 Match the words in the box with the definitions below. Look at A, B and C opposite to help you.

discount rate	discounted cash flow	internal rate of return
purchasing power	rate of return	time value of money

1 a series of future earnings converted to their value today
2 the annual percentage amount of income received from an investment
3 the interest rate an investment earns when the present value of all costs equals the present value of all returns
4 the difference between the value of money held now, and its value if it is received in the future, because it could be invested during that period
5 the value of money, measured by the quantity (and quality) of products and services it can buy
6 the interest rate used to calculate the present value of future cash flows

41.2 Are the following statements true or false? Find reasons for your answers in A and B opposite.

1 If a company uses its own money for a new project, there is no opportunity cost of capital.
2 A project financed by borrowed money requires a rate of return higher than the cost of capital.
3 Because of inflation, money will usually be worth more in the future than at the present.
4 The longer you have to wait for investment returns, the less their present value is.

41.3 Match the two parts of the sentences. Look at B and C opposite to help you.

1 Future cash flows are usually discounted
2 If a project seems to be particularly risky or uncertain,
3 Money you possess now is worth more than money received in the future, because
4 The net present value of a project is the sum of all the returns it is expected to provide,
5 When choosing among potential investments,

a businesses look for the one with the highest internal rate of return.
b by the cost of the capital involved in the investment.
c discounted to their current value.
d it can earn interest in that time, and there might be inflation.
e you can increase the discount rate you use in your calculations.

Over to you

What return can a company get on risk-free investments in your country today? What is the minimum rate of return a company would require on an uncertain new investment?

42 Financial regulation and supervision

A Government regulation

Mei Lee is the **compliance** officer at a large US bank with subsidiaries in major financial centres: she has to make sure that everybody obeys government regulations and follows internal procedures.

'The financial services industry was **deregulated** in the 1980s: lots of government controls were removed to make the market freer and more efficient. But a lot of regulations still exist. We're still regulated and supervised by government agencies. For example, in Britain there's the Financial Services Authority (FSA), and here in the States there's the Federal Reserve (or the Fed) and the Securities and Exchange Commission (SEC).

The Fed supervises banks, and the SEC tries to protect investors by requiring full **disclosure**: it makes sure that public companies make all significant financial information available. And it tries to prevent **fraudulent** or illegal practices in the securities markets, such as companies artificially raising their stock price by using dishonest accounting methods or issuing false information.'

B Internal controls

'I have to make sure no one here does any **insider trading** or **dealing** – buying or selling securities when they have **confidential** or secret information about them. For example our mergers and acquisitions department often has advance information about takeovers. This information is usually **price-sensitive**: if you used it you could make the share price change. This gives the people in M&A huge opportunities for profitable insider dealing, but we try to keep what we call "**Chinese walls**" around departments that have confidential information. This means having strict rules about not using or spreading information.

Another thing I have to deal with is **conflicts of interest** – situations where what is good for one department is not in the best interests of another department. For example, if banks want to win investment banking business from a company, their analysts in the research department could produce inaccurate reports exaggerating the client company's financial situation and prospects. This could lead the fund management and stockbroking departments to buy securities in that company, or recommend them to clients, because of false information.'

C Sarbanes-Oxley

'Because of lots of serious conflicts of interest in banks, the US government passed the Sarbanes-Oxley Act in 2002. This requires research analysts to disclose whether they hold any securities in a company they write a research report about, and whether they have been paid by the company.

Another outcome of Sarbanes-Oxley was the establishment of a board to **oversee** or supervise the auditing of public companies, and to prevent auditors doing non-audit services while they're auditing a company. That's because an auditing firm that is also doing **lucrative** – profitable – consulting work with a company might be tempted not to audit the accounts very carefully, and to ignore evidence of illegal practices or "creative accounting". (See Unit 3)

Another part of my job is making sure no criminal organization uses us for **money laundering** – converting illegal or criminal funds into what looks like **legitimate** or legal income, by passing it through a lot of transactions, companies and bank accounts.'

42.1 Match the words in the box with the definitions below. Look at A, B and C opposite to help you.

compliance	disclosure	fraudulent	insider dealing
money laundering	price-sensitive	oversee	

1 adjective meaning able to influence or change a price
2 behaving according to regulations, rules, policies, procedures, etc.
3 buying or selling stocks when you have confidential information about a company
4 disguising the source of money acquired from criminal activities
5 adjective meaning dishonest and illegal (intending to get money by deceiving people)
6 giving investors and customers all the information they need
7 to watch something to make certain that it is being done correctly

42.2 Match the two parts of the sentences. Look at B and C opposite to help you.

1 Criminal organizations try to hide the origin of illegally received money
2 People with privileged, confidential information about a stock could make money
3 Some banks might try to get business from companies, e.g. issuing stocks and bonds,
4 Some companies might try to make their auditors less rigorous
5 Some companies try to raise their stock price

a by acting on that information and buying and selling the stock.
b by also paying them to do consulting work.
c by moving it through lots of different companies and bank accounts.
d by not following accepted accounting methods or by publishing false information.
e by publishing reports that overstate the companies' financial health.

42.3 Complete the newspaper headlines with words from the box. Look at A, B and C opposite to help you.

Chinese walls	compliance officer	conflicts of interest
deregulation	insider traders	laundering money

1 FSA warns that criminal gangs are still .... through bureaux de change

2 Sarbanes–Oxley has greatly reduced .... for auditing firms, report says

3 Senator says even the smallest financial company needs a ....

4 FSA says it's time to get tough on ....: they are almost never prosecuted

5 Fed says .... not functioning in investment banks: suspicious trading is increasing

6 25 years after .... bankers say there's still too much government control

Over to you

Have there been any major cases of financial institutions breaking the law in your country recently? What happened and what could be done to stop it occurring again?

43 International trade

A Trade

Most economists believe in **free trade** – that people and companies should be able to buy goods from all countries, without any barriers when they cross frontiers.

The **comparative cost principle** is that countries should produce whatever they can make the most cheaply. Countries will raise their **living standards** and income if they specialize in the production of the goods and services in which they have the highest relative **productivity**: the amount of output produced per unit of an input (e.g. raw material, labour).

Countries can have an **absolute advantage** – so that they are the cheapest in the world, or a **comparative advantage** – so that they are only more efficient than some other countries in producing certain goods or services. This can be because they have raw materials, a particular climate, qualified labour (skilled workers), and **economies of scale** – reduced production costs because of large-scale production.

B Balance of payments

Imports are goods or services bought from a foreign country. **Exports** are goods or services sold to a foreign country.

A country that exports more goods than it imports has a positive **balance of trade** or a **trade surplus**. The opposite is a negative balance of trade or a **trade deficit**. Trade in goods is sometimes called **visible** trade. Services such as banking, insurance and tourism are sometimes called **invisible** imports and exports. Adding **invisibles** to the balance of trade gives a country's **balance of payments**.

BrE: visible trade; AmE: merchandise trade

"Good invisible export figures this quarter, sir."

C Protectionism

Governments, unlike most economists, often want to **protect** various areas of the economy. These include agriculture – so that the country is certain to have food – and other **strategic industries** that would be necessary if there was a war and international trade became impossible. Governments also want to protect other industries that provide a lot of jobs.

Many governments impose **tariffs** or import taxes on goods from abroad, to make them more expensive and to encourage people to buy local products instead. However, there are an increasing number of free trade areas, without any import tariffs, in Europe, Asia, Africa and the Americas.

The **World Trade Organization** (**WTO**) tries to encourage free trade and reduce **protectionism**: restricting imports in order to help local products. According to the WTO agreement, countries have to offer the same conditions to all trading partners. The only way a country is allowed to try to restrict imports is by imposing tariffs. Countries should not use import **quotas** – limits to the number of products which can be imported – or other restrictive measures. Various international agreements also forbid **dumping** – selling goods abroad at below cost price in order to destroy or weaken competitors or to earn foreign currency to pay for necessary imports.

43.1 Complete the crossword. Look at A, B and C opposite to help you.

Across

2 Countries that export a lot of oil or manufactured goods tend to have a positive .... (7,2,5)
5 A country exporting more than it imports has a trade .... (7)
6 In a free trade area, governments cannot impose a .... on imports. (6)
8 A limit to the quantity of goods that can be imported is a .... (5)
10 and 9 down Adding trade in services to trade in goods gives you the .... of .... (7,8)
11 Billions of dollars leave the USA every year because the country has a big trade .... (7)
14 Attempting to reduce imports in favour of local production is called .... (13)
15 The import and export of goods is called .... trade. (7)

Down

1 Producing in large quantities becomes cheaper because of economies of .... (5)
3 and 4 If a country can produce something more cheaply than anywhere else in the world it has an .... (8,9)
7 Many economists encourage governments to abolish import taxes and have completely .... (4,5)
9 See 10 across.
11 A number of international agreements make it illegal to .... goods on foreign markets at a price that doesn't give a profit. (4)
12 The comparative .... principle is that countries should make the things they can produce the most cheaply. (4)
13 The .... has established rules of trade between nations. (3)

Over to you

What are your country's major exports and imports? Which industries in your country would find it difficult to compete if there was completely free trade?

44 Exchange rates

A Why exchange rates change

An **exchange rate** is the price at which one currency can be exchanged for another (e.g. how many yen are needed to buy a euro). In theory, exchange rates should be at the level that gives **purchasing power parity (PPP)**. This means that the cost of a given selection of goods and services (e.g. a loaf of bread, a kilowatt of electricity) would be the same in different countries. So if the price level in a country increases because of inflation, its currency should **depreciate** – its exchange rate should go down in order to return to PPP. For example, if inflation increases in the US, the dollar exchange rate should go down so that it takes more dollars to buy the same products in other countries.

In fact, PPP does not work, as exchange rates can change due to **currency speculation** – buying currencies in the hope of making a profit. Financial institutions, companies and rich individuals all buy currencies, looking for high interest rates or short-term capital gains if a currency increases in value or **appreciates**. This means exchange rates change due to speculation rather than PPP. Over 95% of the world's currency transactions are purely **speculative**, and not related to trade. Banks and currency traders make considerable profits from the spread between a currency's buying and selling prices.

B Fixed and floating rates

For 25 years after World War II, the levels of most major currencies were determined by governments. They were **fixed** or **pegged against** the US dollar (e.g. from 1946–67, one pound was worth $2.80), and the dollar was pegged against gold. One dollar was worth one thirty-fifth of an ounce of gold, and the US Federal Reserve guaranteed that they could exchange an ounce of gold for $35. This system was known as **gold convertibility**. These fixed exchange rates could only be adjusted if the International Monetary Fund agreed. Pegging against the dollar ended in 1971, because following inflation in the USA, the Federal Reserve did not have enough gold to guarantee the American currency.

Since the early 1970s, there has been a system of **floating exchange rates** in most western countries. This means that exchange rates are determined by people buying and selling currencies in the foreign exchange markets. A **freely floating exchange rate** means one which is determined by **market forces**: the level of supply and demand. If there are more buyers of a currency than sellers, its price will rise; if there are more sellers, it will fall.

Since the introduction of a **common currency** in 2002, fluctuating exchange rates among many European countries are no longer a problem. But the euro continues to fluctuate against the US dollar, the Japanese yen and other currencies.

C Government intervention

Governments and central banks sometimes try to change the value of their currency. They **intervene** in **exchange markets**, using foreign currency **reserves** to buy their own currency – in order to raise its value – or selling to lower it. The resulting rates are known as **managed floating exchange rates.** But speculators generally have a lot more money than a government has in its reserves of foreign currency, so central banks or governments only have limited power to influence exchange rates.

44.1 Are the following statements true or false? Find reasons for your answers in A and B opposite.

1 Purchasing power parity is a theory that doesn't apply in reality.
2 Inflation should lead to an increase in the value of a country's currency.
3 Speculators buy currencies when they expect their value to increase.
4 Speculators generally sell currencies if their interest rate rises.
5 Currency traders offer different buying and selling prices.
6 A lot more currency is exchanged for buying or selling goods than for speculation.
7 The Federal Reserve will no longer exchange US dollars for gold.
8 Most exchange rates used to be fixed; now they float.
9 If more people want to buy a currency than sell it, its price will go down.

44.2 Complete the table with words from A, B and C opposite and related forms. Put a stress mark in front of the stressed syllable in each word. The first one has been done for you.

Verb	Noun(s)	Noun for people	Adjective
	appreci'ation	–	–
		–	converted
depreciate		–	–
		–	interventionary
			speculative

44.3 Complete the newspaper headlines with the correct forms of words from 44.2 above.

1 **US inflation will cause dollar to .... , economists warn**

2 **Top economists say currency undervalued, call for government to allow it to 5–10%**

3 **Increasing currency .... is making exchange rates more volatile**

4 **Common currency: Economic consultant says .... pound to euro would cost British businesses £12bn**

5 **Chinese experts say the .... betting on revaluation are threatening the economy**

6 ***Central bank not expected to .... in currency crisis***

Over to you

What has happened to the value of your currency in the past few years? What do you think were the probable causes of any changes?

45 Financing international trade

A Documentary credits

A company which sells goods or services to other countries is known as an **exporter**. A company which buys products from other countries is called an **importer**. Payment for imported products is usually by **documentary credit**, also called a **letter of credit**. This is a written promise by a bank to pay a certain amount to the seller, within a fixed period, when the bank receives instructions from the buyer.

Documentary credits have a standard form. They generally contain:

- a short description of the goods
- a list of shipping documents required to obtain payment (see C below)
- a final shipping date
- a final date (or expiration date) for presenting the documents to the bank.

Documentary credits are usually **irrevocable**, meaning that they cannot be changed unless all the parties involved agree. **Irrevocable credits** guarantee that the bank which establishes the letter of credit will pay the seller if the documents are presented within the agreed time.

B Bills of exchange

Another method of payment is a **bill of exchange** or **draft**. This is a payment demand, written or drawn up by an exporter, instructing an importer to pay a specific sum of money at a future date. When the bill matures, the importer pays the money to its bank, which transfers the money to the exporter's bank. This bank then pays the money to the exporter after deducting its charges.

A bank may agree to **endorse** or accept a bill of exchange before it matures. To endorse a bill is to guarantee to pay it if the buyer of goods does not. If a bill is endorsed by a well-known bank, the exporter can sell it at a discount in the financial markets. The discount represents the interest the buyer of the bill could have earned between the date of purchase and the bill's maturity date. When the bill matures, the buyer receives the full amount. This way the exporter gets most of the money immediately, and doesn't have to wait for the buyer to pay the bill.

C Export documents

Exporters have to prepare a number of documents to go with the **shipment** or transportation of goods.

- The **commercial invoice** contains details of the goods: quantity, weight, number of packages, price, terms of delivery, terms of payment, and information about the transportation.
- The **bill of lading** is a document signed by the **carrier** or transporter (e.g. the ship's master) confirming that the goods have been received for shipment; it contains a brief description of the goods and details of where they are going.
- The **insurance certificate** also describes the goods and contains details of how to claim if they are lost or damaged **in transit** – while being transported.
- The **certificate of origin** states where the goods come from.
- **Quality** and **weight certificates**, issued by private inspection and testing companies, may be necessary, confirming that these are the correct goods in the right quantity.
- An **export licence** giving the right to sell particular goods abroad is necessary in some cases.

45.1 Are the following statements true or false? Find reasons for your answers in A, B and C opposite.

1 With a letter of credit, the buyer tells the bank when to pay the seller.
2 Letters of credit are only valid for a certain length of time.
3 An exporter usually has the right to change a letter of credit.
4 The bill of lading confirms that the goods have been delivered to the buyer.
5 With a bill of exchange, the seller can get most of the money before the buyer pays.
6 Bills of exchange are sold at less than 100%, but redeemed at 100% at maturity.

45.2 Put the sequence of events in the correct order. The last stage is b. Look at B opposite to help you.

a A bank accepts or endorses the bill of exchange.
b The accepting bank pays the full value of the bill of exchange to whoever bought it.
c The exporter sells the bill of exchange at a discount on the money market.
d The importer receives the goods and pays its bank.
e The importer's bank transfers the money to the accepting bank.
f The seller or exporter writes a bill of exchange and sends it to the buyer or importer (and ships the goods).

1		2		3		4		5		6	b

45.3 Find verbs in A, B and C opposite that can be used to make word combinations with the nouns below. Then use the correct forms of some of the verbs to complete the sentences.

....
....
.... **a bill of exchange**
....
....

.... **documents**
....
....
....

.... **goods**
....
....
....

1 Exporters can get paid sooner if a bill of exchange is .... by a bank.
2 The bill of lading and the insurance certificate both .... the goods.
3 Exporters .... goods to foreign countries.
4 The transporter .... a document confirming that it has .... the goods.
5 In order to be paid, the exporter has to .... the shipping documents to a specific bank.

Over to you

Which banks in your country specialize in trade finance? Which aspects of trade finance would be the most interesting if you worked in this field?

46 Incoterms

A Transport and additional costs

Companies exporting or importing goods use standard arrangements called **Incoterms** – short for International Commercial Terms, established by the International Chamber of Commerce (ICC) – that state the responsibilities of the buyer and the seller. They determine whether the buyer or the seller will pay the **additional costs** – the costs on top of the cost of the goods. These include transportation or shipment, **documentation** – preparing all the necessary documents, **customs clearance** – completing import documents and paying any import duties or taxes, and transport insurance.

B The E and F terms

There are 13 different Incoterms that can be divided into 4 different groups: an **E Term** (**Departure**), the **F Terms** (**Free, Main Carriage Unpaid**), the **C Terms** (**Main Carriage Paid**), and the **D Terms** (**Delivered/Arrival**). Each group of terms adds more responsibilities to the seller and gives fewer to the buyer.

The E term is **EXW** or **Ex Works**. This means that the buyer collects the goods at the seller's own **premises** – place of business – and arranges insurance against loss or damage to the goods in transit.

In the second group, the **F terms**, the seller delivers the goods to a carrier appointed by the buyer and located in the seller's country. The buyer arranges insurance.

- **FCA** or **Free Carrier** means that the goods are delivered to a named place where the carrier can load them onto a truck, train or aeroplane.
- **FAS – Free Alongside Ship** means that seller delivers the goods to the quay next to the ship in the port.
- **FOB – Free On Board** means that the seller pays for loading the goods onto the ship.

C The C and D terms

In the third group, the **C terms**, the seller arranges and pays for the **carriage** or transportation of the goods, but not for the payment of customs duties and taxes. Transportation of goods is also known as **freight**.

- In **CFR – Cost and Freight** (used for ocean freight) and **CPT – Carriage Paid To ...** (used for air freight and land freight), the buyer is responsible for insurance.
- In the terms **CIF – Cost, Insurance and Freight** (used for ocean freight) and **CIP – Carriage and Insurance Paid To ...** (used for air freight and land freight), the seller arranges and pays for insurance.

In the fourth group, the **D Terms**, the seller pays all the costs involved in transporting the goods to the country of destination, including insurance.

- In **DAF – Delivered At Frontier**, the importer is responsible for preparing the documentation and getting the goods through customs.

If the goods are delivered by ship to a port, the two parties can choose who pays for unloading the goods onto the quay. The two possibilities are:

- **DES – Delivered Ex Ship** – the buyer pays for unloading the goods from the ship
- **DEQ – Delivered Ex Quay** – the seller pays for unloading the goods from the ship to the quay, and for the payment of customs duties and taxes.

If the goods go through customs and are delivered to the buyer, there are two possibilities:

- **DDU – Delivered Duty Unpaid** – the buyer pays any import taxes
- **DDP – Delivered Duty Paid** – the seller pays any import taxes.

46.1 Label the diagram using the abbreviations for Incoterms. Look at A, B and C opposite to help you.

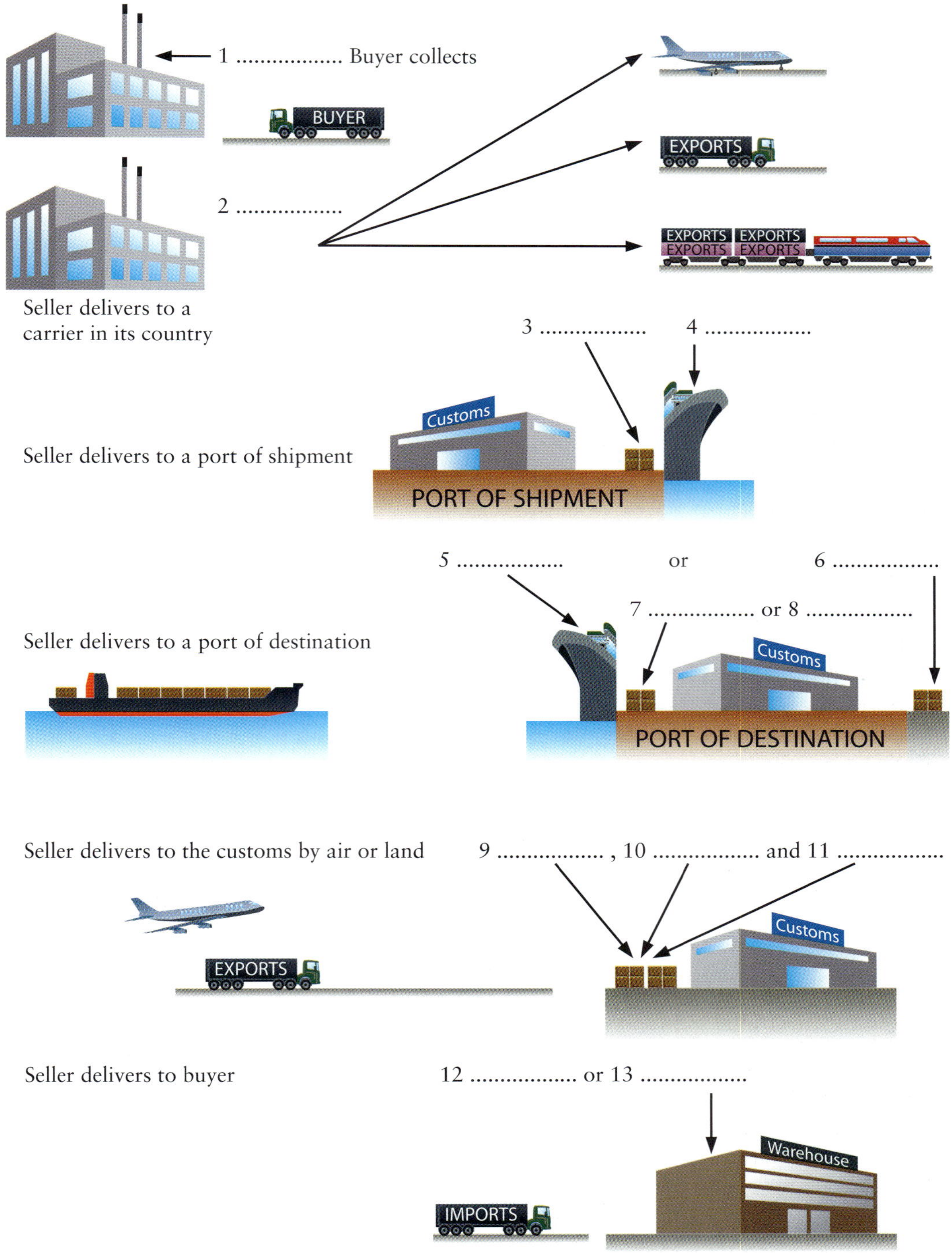

Over to you

How do imported goods normally arrive in your country? Are there taxes on imported products? If you were an importer, would you prefer to organize transport yourself, or let the seller do it?

47 Insurance

A Insuring against risks

Insurance is protection against possible financial **losses**. Individuals, companies and organizations can make regular payments, called **premiums**, to an insurance company which accepts the **risk** (or possibility) of loss. When you buy insurance you make a contract, called a **policy**, with the insurance company – also known as the **insurer**. The contract promises that the company will pay you if you suffer **loss of** or **damage to property**, or **sickness** or **personal injury**.

There are various losses which people or businesses can **insure against**:

- **theft** – someone **stealing** their goods or possessions
- damage from fire or other **natural disasters** such as floods, earthquakes and hurricanes.

If property is stolen or damaged, the person or company who is insured **makes a claim** – requests compensation – from the insurer. The insurer will then **indemnify** or **compensate** them: that is, pay them an amount of money equivalent to the loss. As the number of natural disasters seems to be increasing, so are the claims for damage to property, and this will lead to higher insurance premiums.

In the past, many people buying insurance used independent **brokers** – people who searched for insurance at the lowest cost, or **agents** – people working for the insurance company. But like retail banking, the insurance industry has changed in recent years. A lot of insurance is now sold **direct**, by telephone or on the internet. This can be cheaper than insurance bought **over the counter** from a broker or an agent.

B Life insurance and saving

Life insurance (also called **assurance**) will pay an agreed sum to someone else, for example your husband or wife, if you die before a certain age. People also use life insurance policies as a way to **save** for the future: you can buy a policy that pays a certain sum on a specific date, such as when you retire from work. As with pension plans, life insurance policies are **tax shelters**, or a way of postponing payment of tax. You do not have to pay income tax on life insurance premiums. However a **lump sum** – a single, large amount of money paid out when an insurance policy matures – will be taxable.

C Insurance companies

Insurance companies have to invest the money they receive from premiums. Like pension funds, they are large institutional investors that invest huge sums in securities, especially low-risk ones like government bonds.

The largest insurance market in the world is **Lloyd's of London**. This is an association of people called **underwriters**, who guarantee to indemnify other people's possible losses. Lloyd's spreads risks among a number of **syndicates**: groups of wealthy individuals, commonly known as '**names**'. These people can earn a lot of money from insurance premiums if the clients never claim for compensation, but they also have unlimited **liability** or responsibility for losses.

If insurance companies consider that they have underwritten too many risks, they can sell some of that risk to a **reinsurance** company. This is a company that will receive some of the premium and also **bear**, or take, some of the risk.

47.1 Complete the crossword. Look at A, B and C opposite to help you.

Across

1 and 10 across Some people buy life insurance that pays a .... on retirement. (4,3)

4 Many insurance companies now sell .... , over the phone or the internet. (6)

8 I have a theft policy, so the insurance company will .... me if my mobile phone is stolen. (9)

9 If you make a big claim from your insurance company, the cost of your .... will probably go up. (7)

10 See 1 across.

12 When I insured my house, I used a .... to find me the best deal. (6)

13 Exporters have to insure goods in transit in case somebody .... them. (6)

14 I lost my job as an .... for an insurance company when people stopped buying over the counter. (5)

15 Lloyd's spreads the risks it insures among .... made up of groups of underwriters. (10)

17 The individual underwriters at Lloyd's are commonly called .... (5)

19 Natural disasters are expensive for insurance companies because they cause a lot of .... to buildings and their contents. (6)

Down

2 Lloyd's .... risks worth over £14 billion. (11)

3 You should always read the small print – all the details – before you accept an insurance .... (6)

5 There are .... companies that take on part of the risks underwritten by smaller companies. (11)

6 Life insurance can be a tax .... – a way of putting off paying tax till later. (7)

7 Most people insure their personal .... against loss, fire and theft. (8)

11 .... of London is the world's largest insurance market. (6)

16 Fortunately, I've never had a car accident, so I've never had to .... anything from the insurance company. (5)

18 Life insurance is also a way to .... money and pay less tax. (4)

"Hello, I'd like to apply for some property insurance."

Over to you

How many different insurance policies do you or your family have? Are there any risks you cannot insure yourself against? What insurance does your company or employer have?

48 The business cycle

A Expansion and contraction

All market economies have periods when **consumption** – spending on goods and services – rises. Consumers buy more, companies invest more, and production, income, profits and employment increase. These periods are always followed by periods when spending and investment fall, and unemployment rises. This is the **business cycle.**

A period during which economic activity increases and the economy is expanding is an **upturn** or **upswing.** If it lasts a long time it is called a **boom.** The highest point of the business cycle is a **peak,** which is followed by a **downturn,** during which the amount of economic activity decreases. If the economy keeps contracting for more than six months, the downswing is called a **recession.** A serious, long-lasting recession is called a **depression** or a **slump.** The lowest point of the business cycle is a **trough,** which is followed by a **recovery,** when economic activity increases again, and a new cycle begins.

Note: A **downturn** is also called a **downswing** or a **period of contraction**; a **recovery** is also called an **upturn**, an **upswing** or a **period of expansion**.

B Fiscal policy

Governments and central banks use **fiscal policy,** which involves changing the levels of **government expenditure** and **taxation** to try to limit the extent of the business cycle.

If an economy is moving into a recession, the government might have a **reflationary** fiscal policy. This means trying to **stimulate the economy** by increasing government spending, or by cutting levels of direct or indirect tax so that individuals and companies have more money to spend.

If an economy is **overheating** – expanding too quickly – it means that industry is working at **full capacity** and producing as much as it possibly can. Because demand is greater than supply, leading to rising prices and inflation, the government might have a **deflationary** fiscal policy. This means trying to **cool down the economy**: reducing the amount of economic activity by raising tax rates or cutting government expenditure. This reduces the level of demand in the economy and helps to reduce inflation.

C Monetary policy

Governments or central banks can also use **monetary policy** – changing interest rates and the level of the money supply – to influence the level of economic activity. (See Unit 27) They can **boost** or increase economic activity if the economy is in a downturn by reducing interest rates and allowing the rate of growth of the money supply to increase. Alternatively, if the economy is growing too fast and causing inflation, they can slow it down by increasing interest rates and reducing the rate of growth of the money supply.

The main reason for having an independent central bank (see Unit 23) is to prevent governments from creating a **political business cycle** – a cycle that will be at a high point at the time of the next election. Governments can do this by beginning their periods of office with a couple of years of policies designed to stop the economy from growing, followed by tax cuts and monetary expansion in the two years before the next election. This policy, sometimes called **boom and bust,** helps the government get re-elected but is not good for economic stability. An independent central bank makes this less likely to happen.

48.1 Label the graph with words from the box. Look at A opposite to help you.

boom	downswing	peak	recession	recovery	trough

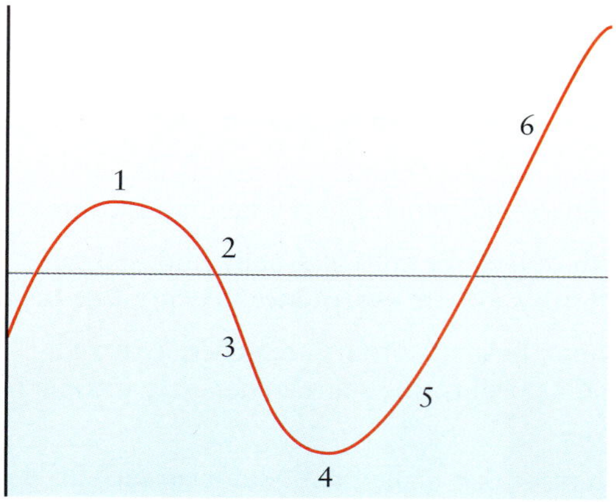

1 ....
2 ....
3 ....
4 ....
5 ....
6 ....

48.2 Match the two parts of the sentences. Look at B and C opposite to help you.

1 If the government thinks the economy is contracting too much,
2 Fiscal policy involves
3 If there isn't an independent central bank, governments can
4 If the government thinks the economy is growing too quickly,
5 Monetary policy involves

a interest rates and the money supply.
b it can raise tax rates and cut its expenditure.
c manipulate the business cycle to their own advantage.
d it can cut taxes and increase its spending.
e taxation and government spending.

48.3 Find verbs in A and B opposite with the following meanings.

to get bigger or make bigger		to get smaller or make smaller	
....	....	....	....
....	....	....	....
....	....	....	....
....	....		

"I've learnt not to worry."

Over to you

Has the economy in your country expanded or contracted over the past three years? What do most economists think were the causes of these changes?

49 Taxation

A Direct taxes

Governments finance most of their expenditure by **taxation**. If they spend more than they **levy** or charge in taxes, they have to borrow money.

Direct taxes are collected by the government from the income of individuals and businesses.

- Individuals pay **income tax** on their wages or salaries, and most other money they receive.
- Most countries have a **capital gains tax** on profits made from the sale of assets such as stocks or shares. This is usually **imposed** or levied at a much lower rate than income tax.
- A **capital transfer tax** (commonly called **death duty** in Britain) is usually imposed on inherited money or property. Other names for this tax are **inheritance tax** or **estate tax**.
- Companies pay **corporation tax** on their profits. Business profits are generally taxed twice, because after the company pays tax on its profits, the shareholders pay income tax on any dividends received from these profits.
- Companies and their employees also have to pay taxes (called **national insurance** in Britain) which the government uses to finance **social security** spending – unemployment pay, sick pay, etc.

BrE: corporation tax; AmE: income tax

B Indirect taxes

Indirect taxes are levied on the production or sale of goods and services. They are included in the price paid by the final purchaser.

- In most European countries, companies pay **VAT** or **value-added tax**, which is levied at each stage of production, based on the value added to the product at that stage. The whole amount is added to the final price paid by the consumer. In Canada, Australia, New Zealand and Singapore, this tax is called **goods and services tax** or **GST**.
- In the USA, there are **sales taxes**, collected by retailers, levied on the retail price of goods.
- Governments also levy **excise taxes** or **excise duties** – additional sales taxes on commodities like tobacco products, alcoholic drinks and petrol.
- Special taxes, called **tariffs**, are often charged on goods imported from abroad. (See Unit 43)

Income tax for individuals is usually **progressive**: people with higher incomes pay a higher rate of tax (and therefore a higher percentage of their income) than people with lower incomes. Indirect taxes such as sales tax and VAT are called **proportional** taxes, imposed at a fixed rate. But indirect taxes are actually **regressive**: people with a low income pay a proportionally greater part of their income than people with a high income.

BrE: petrol; AmE: gasoline

C Non-payment of tax

To reduce the amount of income tax that employees have to pay, some employers give their staff advantages instead of taxable money, called **perks**, such as company cars and free health insurance.

Multinational companies often register their head offices in **tax havens** – small countries where income taxes for foreign companies are low, such as Liechtenstein, Monaco, the Cayman Islands, and the Bahamas.

Using legal methods to minimize your **tax burden** – the amount of tax you have to pay – is called **tax avoidance**. This often involves using **loopholes** – ways of getting around the law, because of an error or a technicality in the law itself. Using illegal methods – such as not declaring your income, or reporting it inaccurately – is called **tax evasion**, and can lead to big penalties.

49.1 What are the standard names for the tax or taxes paid on the following? Look at A and B opposite to help you.

1 alcoholic drinks and tobacco products
2 company profits
3 goods bought in stores
4 money received from relatives after their death
5 salaries and wages
6 goods made in other countries
7 money made by selling stocks at a profit

49.2 Find words in A and B opposite with the following meanings.

1 an adjective describing taxes on revenue or income
2 a tax that has one rate that is the same for everybody
3 money paid by the government to sick and unemployed people
4 a tax that has a higher rate for taxpayers with a higher income
5 an adjective describing taxes on consumption or spending

49.3 Are the following statements true or false? Find reasons for your answers in A, B and C opposite.

1 Capital gains are generally taxed at a higher rate than income.
2 The same sum of money can be taxed more than once.
3 Sales taxes can be both proportional and progressive at the same time.
4 Excise duties are extra sales taxes on selected products.
5 Many international companies have their registered headquarters in small countries where they do only a small proportion of their business.
6 Employees will generally pay less tax if their employer reduces their salary a little and provides them with a car.
7 Tax avoidance is illegal.
8 Perks and loopholes are forms of tax evasion.

49.4 Find five verbs in A and B opposite that can be used to make word combinations with 'tax'.

....
....
.... **tax**
....
....

Over to you

In your country, what percentage of national income goes to the government as tax? Do you know how this compares with other countries?

50 Business plans

A Market opportunities

If you have a brilliant idea for a new product or service, or a better or cheaper way of supplying an existing product or service, you will probably require finance: money to start up a company to take this **market opportunity**, or to expand an existing company. If you want to interest venture capitalists (see Unit 28) in your project, you will have to write a **business plan**.

Business plans begin with a summary, often called an **Executive Summary**, which explains in one or two pages:

- what sort of company it is
- what the product or service is, and what is special about it
- who the managers are
- how much money you need, and what you will use it for.

B The company, the product and the market

If the company already exists, the first chapter of the business plan explains how it was started and how it has grown, and gives a history of sales and profits. It describes the company today, and the plans for the future.

The second chapter describes what you already sell or want to sell. It explains what differentiates the product or service from other existing ones – what makes it different or **unique**. It focuses on the **benefits** or advantages for customers – how it will improve people's lives!

The chapter on the market describes the industry you operate in, the market segments, the other firms in the market (your competitors), changes in the industry, and **projected trends** – forecasts for the future – and technological opportunities. It outlines what the customers need, where they are, and how you plan to reach them. It explains how you will make sure that customers know about your product or service and why they will prefer it to the competition. It gives details of your **marketing strategy**, including sales **tactics** – the ways you plan to achieve sales, advertising, publicity and **sales promotions** – incentives to encourage customers to buy.

The chapter on the management team gives details about the most important staff. The chapter on strategy outlines your strategies for marketing, pricing, distribution, sales, etc., and how you are going to **implement** them or carry them out.

C The financial analysis

The financial analysis gives details of the historical performance, if it is an existing company, and describes existing finance and assets. It explains why the business needs funds, and gives **sales forecasts** (the sales the business expects to achieve in a particular period of time), projected or expected financial statements (profit and loss account, cash flow statement, and balance sheet), and projections for future income. It will probably include a breakeven analysis, and an analysis of financial ratios.

Various appendices can come at the end of the business plan, including the **curriculum vitae** (CV) of each top manager and promotional materials for your products.

BrE: curriculum vitae; AmE: résumé

50.1 Make word combinations using a word from each box. Then use the word combinations to complete the sentences below. Look at A and B opposite to help you.

implement reach require supply	customers finance services strategies

1 Are you sure you can .... these .... more efficiently than your competitors?
2 This business plan gives details of the .... we .... , and what we're going to do with it.
3 We'll hire two experienced managers to help us .... our ....
4 We're convinced our innovative advertising will allow us to .... our potential ....

50.2 Complete the sentences. Look at A, B and C opposite to help you.

1 We're convinced this is a great .... : people will really want what we plan to offer.

2 Our .... is over 100,000 units a year.

3 The product is .... : there's absolutely nothing else like it on the market.

4 Our .... is essentially to advertise a lot and sell at a very low price.

5 The advertising will stress the .... the consumers will get from the product – how it will save them time and money.

6 We'll also use a few .... , such as giving away free samples or offering discounts.

50.3 Use the words below to make word combinations with 'market' that have appeared in this book. Then sort the word combinations: which are concerned with finance and which with marketing?

market

bear, value, capitalization, stock, currency, skimming, equity, share, maker, segment, over-the-counter, price, secondary, primary, penetration

Over to you

If you were starting up a new company, what product or service would it offer? What would you include in your business plan to try to convince venture capitalists to invest?

Language reference – market idioms

Financial journalists and people working in finance use lots of different expressions to describe price changes in financial markets. These are the most common ones. (Some of these words also appear in Unit 38.)

Small or slow upward movement

Verbs	
to advance	to gain
to firm	to be a little stronger
to be firm	to be slightly stronger
to be firmer	

Large upward movement

Verbs		Nouns
to jump	to soar	a jump
to leap	to strengthen	a leap
to rocket	to surge	
to shoot up	to take off	
to skyrocket		

Upward movement following previous downward movement

Verbs	Nouns
to stage a comeback	a comeback
to rebound	a rally
to recover	a rebound
to revive	a recovery
to rally	

Small or slow downward movement

Verbs		Nouns
to dip	to lower	a decline
to decline	to slide	a slide
to drift down	to ease	
to weaken		
to slip or slip back		
to be or come under pressure		

Large downward movement

Verbs			Nouns
to crash	to dive	to drop	a crash
to sink	to skid	to slump	a dive
to plummet	to fall sharply		a drop
to go south			
to go or fall through the floor			
to plunge or take a plunge			
to suffer a drop or a setback			
to take a beating or a knock			
to tumble or take a tumble			

No change

Verbs	
to be or remain steady or stable	to be or remain unchanged

Note: Some verbs have irregular past forms, for example *leap – leapt – leapt*; *shoot – shot – shot*; *fall – fell – fallen.*

Language reference – numbers

Saying and writing numbers

Everyone working in finance uses a lot of numbers. Saying and understanding numbers or figures in a foreign language can be difficult.

This is how numbers above 100 are said, and written in legal contracts and on cheques:

100	a hundred *or* one hundred
200	two hundred (*not* two hundreds)
1,000	a/one thousand
1,100	a/one thousand one hundred *or* eleven hundred
1,234	a/one thousand two hundred and thirty-four *or* twelve hundred and thirty-four
2,200	two thousand two hundred
100,000	a/one hundred thousand
1,000,000	a/one million
1,000,000,000	a/one billion
1,000,000,000,000	a/one trillion

BrE: uses 'and' in figures – a hundred and twenty-five thousand;
AmE: doesn't use 'and' in figures – a hundred twenty-five thousand

English uses a **comma** (,) to separate large numbers into groups of three digits, counting from the right.

12,345	twelve thousand, three hundred and forty-five
12,345,678	twelve million, three hundred and forty-five thousand, six hundred and seventy-eight.

Note: English does not use a raised comma (12'345).

Saying amounts of currency

The name of a currency is said *after* the number (or in the middle of the number), but is written *before* the number.

€10	ten euros
$10.95	ten dollars ninety-five
¥50,000	fifty thousand yen
£3.50	three pounds fifty *or* three fifty

The smaller currency unit (e.g. cents or pence) is not usually said.

Decimals

English uses a **point** (.) for **decimal** numbers. The numbers before a decimal point are said normally. All the digits after a decimal point are said separately.

1.25	one point two five
12.45	twelve point four five
3.14159	three point one four one five nine

If the decimal is a unit (of money, for example), both parts can be said like normal numbers.

87.65	eighty-seven point six five
$87.65	The stock is trading at eighty-seven sixty-five.

Fractions

$^{1}/_{2}$	a half	$^{5}/_{16}$	five sixteenths
$^{1}/_{3}$	a third / one third	$^{7}/_{32}$	seven thirty-seconds
$^{1}/_{4}$	a quarter / one quarter	$1^{1}/_{2}$	one and a half
$^{3}/_{4}$	three quarters	$2^{2}/_{3}$	two and two thirds
$^{1}/_{5}$	a fifth		

BrE: a quarter;
AmE: a quarter, a fourth

Ordinals

To put things in an order, use **ordinal numbers.**

1st	(the) first	60th	(the) sixtieth
2nd	(the) second	61st	(the) sixty-first
3rd	(the) third	62nd	(the) sixty-second
4th	(the) fourth	100th	(the) hundredth
5th	(the) fifth	1,000th	(the) thousandth
6th	(the) sixth		

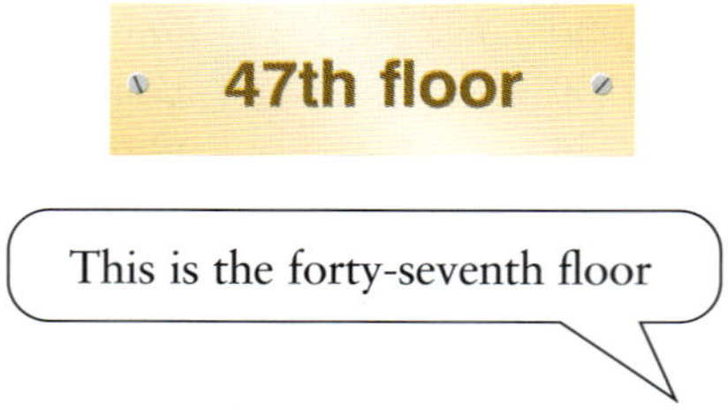

Saying sequences of numbers

0 is called **zero** (or sometimes in Britain, **nought**).

After a decimal point and in telephone numbers, room numbers, bus numbers, etc., British English uses **oh.**

room seven oh four

the one oh six bus

For telephone numbers, fax numbers, bank account numbers, credit card numbers, passport numbers, etc., people usually say each digit separately, but in groups of two, three or four digits.

0202-456-1414 oh two oh two, four five six, one four one four

BrE: oh; AmE: zero

An exception is double numbers:

0255-226-3344 oh two double five, double two six, double three double four

BrE: double oh; AmE: zero zero

A rising intonation is used at the end of each group of numbers except the last one, which has a falling tone, showing that the end of the number has been reached.

↗ 00 ↗ 44 ↗ 1223 ↗ 325 ↘ 566

Numbers as adjectives

When a number is used as part of an **adjective,** it is always **singular** (i.e. it doesn't have an *-s* at the end).

a twenty-minute walk	a four-syllable word	a ten-thousand euro bonus
a two-hour flight	a five-person team	a fifty-thousand dollar car
a three-day holiday	a six-figure number	

If you find saying long numbers difficult, practise reading numbers aloud from a business newspaper, or using your personal documents, telephone book, etc.

Language reference – word stress

Long words can be divided into different parts, each of which is a unit of pronunciation. These units are called syllables. The word *syl·la·ble* has three syllables, *u·nit* has two, *pro·nun·ci·a·tion* has five.

In spoken English, syllables are either stressed or unstressed (or accented and unaccented). In the following examples the syllable following the (') mark is stressed.

- One syllable of nouns (*'business*), verbs (*in'vest*), adjectives (*ex'pensive*) and adverbs (*'quickly*) is **stressed.**
- Prepositions (*in*, *at*, *to*), pronouns (*he*, *me*), and articles (*a*, *the*) are usually **unstressed.**

1 The usual rule for **two-syllable** words is to stress the first syllable.
'asset *'budget* *'credit*

2 Most **three-syllable** words are also stressed on the first syllable.
'auditor *'capital* *'corporate*

3 Most words of **four or more syllables** are stressed on the third syllable from the end.
col'lateral *e'conomy* *lia'bilities*

4 Because not all syllables are pronounced in English, some words which look like they have three syllables are reduced to two, and some words which look like they have four syllables are reduced to three. This means that these words are stressed on the first syllable. In the examples below, the letters marked [ ] are not pronounced.

bus[i]ness *int[e]rest* *int[e]resting* *secret[a]ry* *diction[a]ry*

5 However, there are lots of **exceptions** to these rules. The most common one is that most (Latin) **prefixes** are not stressed, but even this rule has an exception since the *pre-* in 'prefix' <u>is</u> stressed.

co-	*col'lect*	con-	*con'nect*	pre-	*pre'dict*
com-	*com'ponent*	ex-	*ex'pect*	pro-	*pro'vide*

6 There is a large group of two-syllable words which are both a noun and a verb, or an adjective and a verb, which are stressed on the **first** syllable of the **noun** or **adjective**, and the **second** syllable of the **verb.**

We're looking for 'finance – we need someone to fi'nance the company.
We're using a new 'transport company to trans'port the goods from China.

Two-syllable words that follow this stress pattern include:

conduct	*decrease*	*increase*	*refund*
conflict	*discount*	*permit*	*reject*
contrast	*export*	*present*	*survey*
convert	*import*	*produce*	*transfer*

Because of this rule, and the large number of verbs that begin with a prefix, more two-syllable verbs are stressed on the second syllable than the first (despite rule 1 above).

Where these words are also **adjectives** (*a 'perfect product, an 'import barrier*), they are stressed like the noun. Where the adjective is the same as the past participle of the verb (*per'fected, im'ported*), it is stressed on the second syllable, like the verb.

7 Most **suffixes** are unstressed. Exceptions include:

-ation	*allo'cation*	*depreci'ation*	*integ'ration*
-ition	*po'sition*	*acqui'sition*	*con'ditional*
-otion	*pro'motion*	*pro'motional*	
-ution	*insti'tution*	*so'lution*	*distri'bution*
-ee	*employ'ee*	*trai'nee*	*guaran'tee*
-eer	*car'eer*	*engin'eer*	

Suffixes do not normally change the three-syllable rule, so *'advertising* and *'organizer* are stressed on the first syllable, although they are four-syllable words.

8 There are various regular patterns of syllables (often at the end of a word) that come just *after* a stressed syllable.

- Most words ending in *-ic*, *-ical* and *-ically* are stressed on the previous syllable.
  auto'matic *eco'nomic* *his'torical* *syste'matically*
- Most words ending in *-ial*, *-ially*, *-ual*, and *-ually* are stressed on the previous syllable.
  com'mercial *fi'nancially* *'annual* *indi'vidually*
- Most words ending in *-ible*, *-ity* and *-ify* are stressed on the previous syllable.
  con'vertible *converti'bility* *di'versify*
- Most words ending in *-ious*, *-eous* and *-uous* are stressed on the previous syllable.
  'obvious *simul'taneous* *am'biguous*

9 The last letter of a group of initials is usually stressed.

AG'M *AT'M* *EP'S* *IP'O* *LB'O* *OT'C* *PL'C* *US'A* *VA'T*

Language reference – British and American vocabulary

British English	American English
aluminium	aluminum
Annual General Meeting (AGM)	Annual Meeting of Stockholders
Articles of Association	Bylaws
balance sheet	balance sheet / statement of financial position
base rate	prime rate
building society	savings and loans association
cash dispenser	ATM (Automated Teller Machine)
chairman	president
cheque	check
convertible share	convertible bond
corporation tax	income tax
cost centre	cost center
creditors	accounts payable
current account	checking account
debtors	accounts receivable
depreciation	depreciation / amortization
Extraordinary General Meeting (EGM)	Special Meeting
financial year	fiscal year
fixed assets	property, plant and equipment
flat	apartment
flotation	initial public offering (IPO)
gearing	leverage
index-linked fund	tracker fund
labour	labor
managing director	chief executive officer (CEO)
Memorandum of Association	Certificate of Incorporation
merchant bank	investment bank
net profit	net income
note or banknote	bill
ordinary shares	common stock
overheads	overhead
own shares	treasury stock
petrol	gasoline
PLC	listed company
preference shares	preferred stock
profit and loss account	income statement
shareholder	stockholder
shareholders' equity	stockholders' equity
shares	stocks
shopping centre	shopping mall
social security	welfare
stock	inventory
stock take	count of the inventory
traveller's cheque	traveler's check
true and fair view	fair presentation
visible trade	merchandise trade

Answer key

1.1 1 social security, salary
2 earn, commission
3 bonus
4 mortgage
5 currency
6 overtime
7 tax
8 rent
9 pension

1.2 1 false – most money … consists of bank deposits
2 true – salaries are usually paid monthly and wages are usually paid weekly
3 false – commission is a percentage of the income they generate, which can change
4 true – money paid by a company or the government to a retired person is a pension
5 false – most people pay one or the other, depending on whether they are buying or renting their home

2.1

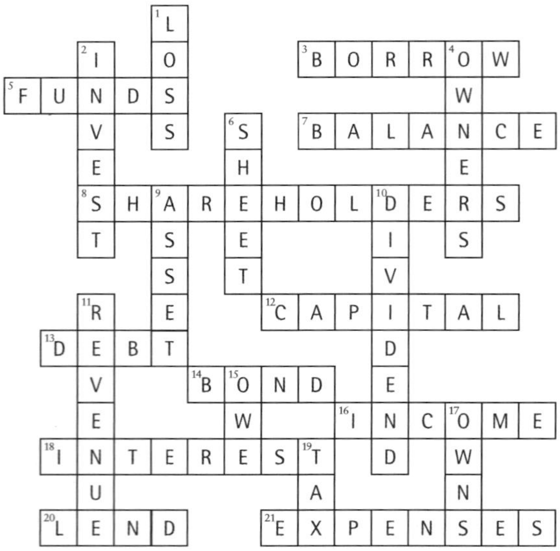

3.1 1 bookkeeping, a bookkeeper
2 external auditing, an independent auditor
3 management accounting, a management accountant
4 financial accounting, a financial accountant
5 accounting, an accountant / internal auditing, an internal auditor

3.2 1c, 2e, 3a, 4b, 5d

3.3 carry out an audit
do an audit
establish rules
follow rules
make rules
set rules
apply standards
establish standards
use standards
record transactions
summarize transactions

4.1 1 debit
2 ledger
3 debtors
4 credit
5 stock
6 creditors

4.2 1 Double-entry bookkeeping, account, debit
2 day books, journals
3 nominal ledgers, bought ledger
4 trial balance

4.3 1 debit 3 debit, credit
2 debit 4 credit, debit

5.1 1 false – a company ... has a separate legal existence from its owners, the shareholders
2 false – the owners are not fully liable for – or responsible for – the business's debts ... Their liability is limited to the value of their share capital
3 true – managers and executive directors run the company for its owners
4 true – Non-executive directors are often more objective
5 false – partners are fully liable or responsible for any debts the business has
6 false – partnerships are not legal entities, so in case of a legal action, it is the individual partners and not the partnership that is taken to court

5.2 corporate governance
audit committee
limited liability
non-executive directors
share capital

1 audit committee 4 limited liability
2 non-executive directors 5 corporate governance
3 share capital

5.3 a Memorandum c purpose
b registered office d authorized share capital

6.1 1 private 4 quoted 7 quarterly
2 stock exchange 5 interim 8 annual report
3 limited 6 listed 9 AGM

6.2 1 misconduct 3 net profit
2 gross profit 4 turnover

6.3 1e, 2a, 3b, 4c, 5f, 6d

7.1 1c, 2e, 3d, 4a, 5b

7.2 1 false – Companies can choose their accounting policies ... There are a range of methods of valuation ... and measurement
2 false – accounting policies ... have to be consistent, which means using the same methods every year, unless there is a good reason to change a policy
3 true – Areas in which the choice of policies can make a big difference include depreciation ... [and] the valuation of stock or inventory
4 false – companies have to give a true and fair view of their financial situation – meaning there are various possibilities – rather than <u>the</u> true and fair view – meaning only one is possible
5 true – in many countries accounting follows the historical cost principle: the original purchase price of assets is recorded in accounts, and not their (estimated) current selling price
6 true – some countries with regular high inflation ... use inflation accounting systems that take account of changing prices

7.3

Verb	Noun(s)	Adjective
'calculate	calcu'lation	–
–	con'sistency	con'sistent
–	con'vention	con'ventional
'measure	'measurement	–
pre'sent	presen'tation	–
'value	'value, valu'ation	'valuable

8.1 1f, 2d, 3e, 4c, 5b, 6a

8.2
1 financial year / fiscal year
2 subsidiary
3 consolidated financial statements
4 verifiable

8.3

Verb	Noun	Adjective
as'sume	as'sumption	–
dis'close	dis'closure	–
–	objec'tivity	ob'jective
'recognize	recog'nition	–
–	subjec'tivity	sub'jective
'verify	verifi'cation	'verifiable

1 verify
2 disclose
3 objectivity
4 assume

9.1
1 revalue
2 current assets
3 appreciate
4 obsolete
5 fixed assets
6 wear out

9.2
deduct costs
depreciate fixed assets
record market value
record purchase price
reduce profits
reduce value

1 record, purchase price
2 fixed assets, deduct, costs
3 reduce, value

9.3 1e, 2c, 3a, 4b, 5d

10.1 1d, 2c, 3a, 4b

10.2 check accounts
check stock take
check systems of control
comply with laws
comply with policies
comply with procedures
comply with regulations
examine accounts
examine systems of control
give advice
give opinions

10.3

Verb	Noun	Adjective
–	'accuracy	'accurate
com'ply	com'pliance	–
recom'mend	recommen'dation	recom'mended
re'cord	'record	–
ex'amine	exami'nation	–

1 examine, accurate, comply
2 recommendations
3 recorded

11.1
1 true – American and continental European companies usually put assets on the left and capital and liabilities on the right ... most British companies use a vertical format, with assets at the top, and liabilities and capital below
2 false – A balance sheet does not show how much money a company has spent or received during a year
3 true – Since assets are shown as debits ... and the total must correspond with the total sum of the credits ... assets equal liabilities plus capital (or A = L + C)
4 true – shows the company's liabilities, and its capital or shareholders' equity ... Part of this is share capital – the money the company raised by selling its shares
5 false – assets equal liabilities plus capital
6 true – Liabilities are obligations to pay other organizations or people: money that the company owes, or will owe at a future date

11.2
1 Suppliers
2 Retained earnings
3 Assets
4 Liabilities
5 Shareholders' equity

11.3 distribute profits
grant credit
owe money
pay liabilities
retain earnings

1 retain, earnings, distribute, profits
2 owe money, grant, credit
3 liabilities, pay

12.1

1 bad debt
2 net worth / net assets
3 patent
4 net book value
5 goodwill
6 trade mark
7 write off
8 to make provisions
9 work-in-progress
10 debtors / accounts receivable

12.2 1e, 2b, 3a, 4f, 5d, 6c

12.3 Current assets: cash in the bank, debtors, stock
Fixed assets: buildings, land, investments
Intangible assets: goodwill, human capital, reputation

13.1

1 false – Current liabilities are expected to be paid within a year of the date of the balance sheet (if it has been paid, it is no longer a liability and will not appear on the balance sheet)
2 true – current is defined as within a year of the date of the balance sheet
3 true – accrued expenses are charged against income – that is, deducted from profits – even though the bills have not yet been received or the cash paid
4 true – Shareholders' equity includes: the original share capital ... share premium: money made if the company sells shares at above their face value – the value written on them ... retained earnings
5 false – shareholders' equity includes retained earnings – it is money belonging to the shareholders and not the company
6 true – share premium is money made if the company sells shares at above their face value – the value written on them

13.2

1 current liabilities
2 share premium
3 deferred
4 accrued

13.3 Assets: Accounts receivable, Cash and equivalents, Inventory, Investments, Land and buildings
Liabilities: Accounts payable, Accrued expenses, Deferred taxes, Dividends, Long-term debt

14.1

1 sales revenue
2 gross profit
3 EBITDA
4 pre-tax income
5 net profit

14.2

1 Operations
2 Investing
3 Financing
4 operations
5 financing
6 operations
7 investing

14.3 Operating activities: Changes in operating assets and liabilities, Depreciation and amortization expenses, Income taxes payable, Net income
Financing activities: Dividends paid, Issuance of stock, Payments to repurchase stock, Repayment of debt
Investing activities: Purchase of plant and equipment, Sale of property

15.1

1 liquidity
2 efficiency
3 ratio
4 solvency

15.2 acid test
current ratio
dividend cover
liquid assets
quick ratio

1 liquid assets
2 dividend cover
3 acid test, quick ratio
4 current ratio

15.3 1b, 2d, 3a, 4c

16.1 1c, 2a, 3b, 4d

16.2 1 D, 2 E, 3 A, 4 C, 5 B

17.1
1 overheads
2 cost centre
3 variable costs
4 profitable
5 fixed costs
6 breakeven point

17.2

Cost	Direct	Indirect	Fixed	Variable
Advertising expenses		✓		✓
Bad debts		✓		✓
Components	✓			✓
Electricity to run machines	✓			✓
Electricity for heating		✓		✓
Equipment repairs		✓		✓
Factory canteen		✓	✓	
Overtime pay	✓			✓
Raw materials	✓			✓
Property tax		✓	✓	
Rent		✓	✓	

17.3 1a, 2b

18.1 charge prices
cut prices
lower prices
pay prices
raise prices

1 cut/lower
2 raise
3 pay
4 charge
5 cut/lower

18.2
1 prestige pricing
2 odd pricing
3 market skimming
4 mark-up pricing
5 going-rate pricing
6 loss-leader pricing
7 market penetration

19.1
1 current accounts
2 savings accounts
3 debit card
4 credit card
5 standing order
6 direct debit
7 statements
8 foreign currency
9 traveller's cheques

19.2
1 interest
2 loan
3 collateral
4 overdraft
5 mortgage
6 private pension plan
7 repossess

19.3
1 false – a savings account or deposit account … pays more interest
2 true – If the borrower doesn't repay the mortgage, the bank can repossess the house or flat
3 true – traveller's cheques … are protected against loss or theft
4 true – Commercial banks … discovered that most of their customers preferred to go to branches
5 false – customers preferred to go to branches … especially ones … which were conveniently situated in shopping centres (but not all branches are)

20.1
1 bank account
2 corporate customers
3 grant loans
4 conditions, personal customers

20.2
1f, 2e, 3b, 4a, 5c, 6d

20.3
charge interest
pay interest
transfer money
withdraw money
assess risks
calculate risks

1 charged
2 withdraw
3 assess

21.1
1 financial institution
2 capital
3 merger
4 conglomerate
5 deregulation
6 takeover bid

21.2
1 investment/merchant banks
2 insurance companies
3 investment/merchant banks
4 building societies / savings and loans associations
5 commercial/retail/High Street banks
6 investment/merchant banks
7 investment/merchant banks
8 insurance companies

21.3
1 central bank
2 investment bank
3 private bank
4 clearing bank
5 retail/commercial/High Street bank

22.1

Verb	Noun(s)	Noun for people	Adjective(s)
a'cquire	acqui'sition	–	–
ad'vise	ad'vice	ad'viser or ad'visor	–
'analyse	a'nalysis	'analyst	ana'lytic, ana'lytical
'institute	insti'tution	–	insti'tutional
in'vest	in'vestment	in'vestor	–
'value	'value, valu'ation	–	'valuable

22.2
1 underwritten
2 advised
3 divesting, acquiring
4 fees
5 merged
6 IPOs

22.3
1 consulting firm
2 pension fund
3 strategic planning
4 forecasters
5 subsidiary
6 institutional investor
7 financial restructuring
8 valuation

23.1 1b, 2a, 3d, 4e, 5c

23.2
a monetary
b supervising
c stability
d financial

23.3
bank run
currency markets
exchange rate
financial system
financial stability
monetary policy

1 monetary policy, financial stability
2 bank run, financial system
3 currency markets, exchange rate

24.1
1 interest rate
2 solvency
3 labour
4 floating rate
5 creditworthy
6 spread
7 output
8 invest

24.2
1 e discount rate
2 c base rate or prime rate
3 a mortgage
4 d overdraft
5 b hire purchase

24.3
1 false – The discount rate is the rate that the central bank sets … When this rate changes, the commercial banks change their own base rate … This is the rate from which they calculate all their other deposit and lending rates
2 true – When interest rates fall, people borrow more, and spend rather than save
3 false – The higher the borrower's solvency, the lower the interest rate they pay
4 true – Borrowers can usually get a lower interest rate if the loan is guaranteed by securities or other collateral
5 true – The rate that borrowers pay depends on their creditworthiness … The higher the borrower's solvency, the lower the interest rate they pay (the bigger the risk, the higher the interest rate)
6 true – mortgages often have floating or variable interest rates that change according to the supply and demand for money

25.1
1 true – a business or government that needs cash for a few weeks only can use the money market
2 false – to borrow or invest short-term capital
3 false – T-bills are ... usually sold at a discount ... rather than paying interest ... Commercial paper is ... also sold at a discount
4 false – Certificates of deposit are issued by banks
5 false – Commercial paper ... is unsecured
6 true – Certificates of deposit ... are issued by banks to large depositors who can then trade them in the short-term money markets

25.2
1 discount
2 competitive
3 liquidity
4 short-term
5 unsecured
6 redeemed
7 maturity
8 cash flow
9 par value

25.3 1b, 2c, 3a, 4e, 5d

26.1 1d, 2c, 3a, 4b, 5e

26.2 Customers of Islamic banks: 2, 3, 5
Customer of conventional banks: 1, 4

26.3 investment account
service charge
risk capitalists
working captial

1 working capital
2 service charge
3 risk capitalists
4 investment account

27.1
1 true – currency in circulation ... makes up only a very small part of the money supply. The rest consists of bank deposits
2 false – time deposits [are] bank deposits that can only be withdrawn after a certain period of time
3 true – To measure money you also have to know how often it is spent in a given period ... the quantity of money spent is the money supply times its velocity of circulation
4 true – the central bank ... use[s] monetary policy to try to control the amount of money in circulation, and its growth
5 false – [the monetary authorities] can change commercial banks' reserve–asset ratio ... the percentage of deposits a bank has to keep in its reserves

27.2 broad money
money supply
narrow money

1 money supply
2 narrow money
3 Broad money

27.3
1 monetary authorities
2 monetary policy
3 monetary growth

28.1

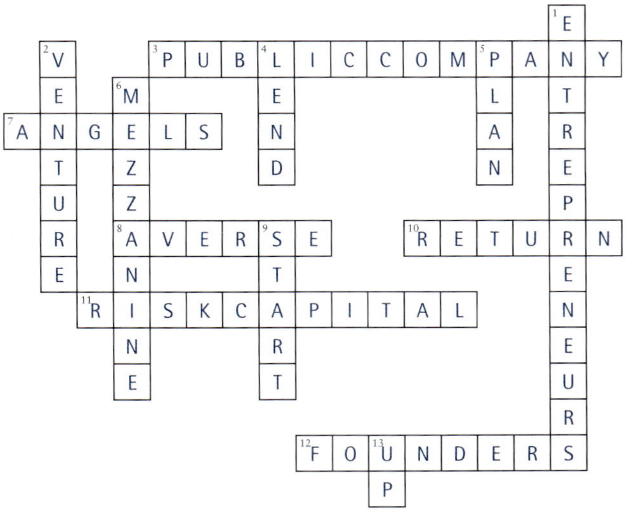

28.2 1e, 2f, 3b, 4a, 5d, 6c

29.1

1 prospectus
2 stock exchange
3 investors
4 going public
5 flotation
6 to underwrite
7 preference shares
8 ordinary shares
9 bankrupt
10 liquidation

29.2

1 false – only successful existing companies can go public
2 true – An investment bank underwrites the stock issue: guarantees to buy the shares if there are not enough other buyers
3 false – The company gets independent accountants to produce a due diligence report
4 false – preference shares ... holders receive a fixed dividend
5 false – holders of preference shares are repaid before other shareholders, but after owners of bonds and other debts

29.3

offer shares
go public
produce a prospectus
underwrite an issue

1 go
2 public
3 offering
4 shares
5 produced
6 prospectus
7 underwriting
8 issue

30.1

1 rights issue
2 nominal value
3 to capitalize
4 secondary market
5 market price
6 own shares
7 primary market

30.2

1 false – newly issued shares [are] sold for the first time [on] the primary market
2 false – over-the-counter markets such as NASDAQ ... and AIM ... have fewer regulations
3 true – market price ... depends on supply and demand – how many sellers and buyers there are
4 true – automatic trading systems ... match up buyers and sellers
5 true – The spread or difference between these prices is their profit or mark-up

30.3
1 value stock
2 defensive stocks
3 blue chips
4 growth stocks
5 income stock
6 rights issue
7 scrip/capitalization/bonus issue
8 own shares

31.1
1 bear market
2 bull market
3 crash

31.2 Possible answers:
1 They buy stocks in issues that are over-subscribed, so they can immediately re-sell them at a profit.
2 Because if a company makes a profit but does not pay dividends, its stock price will rise, and stockholders can make a capital gain by selling the stocks. Capital gains are taxed at a lower rate than dividends, which are income.
3 By agreeing to sell something at a fixed price, and then buying it at a lower price.

31.3
make a capital gain
make a profit
own securities
pay a dividend
pay tax
receive a dividend
retain earnings
take a position

1 pay, tax, receive, dividend, retains, earnings, make, capital gain
2 make, profit, taking, position, securities, own

32.1 1d, 2b, 3a, 4c

32.2
1 false – Fundamental analysis ... ignores the behaviour of investors and assumes that a share has a true or correct value
2 true – Fundamental analysis ... assumes that a share has a true or correct value, which ... reflects the present value of the future income from dividends
3 true – Investors can reduce these by having a diversified portfolio
4 false – Unsystematic risks are things that affect individual companies (and their shares)

32.3 1b, 2c, 3a

33.1
1 principal
2 credit rating
3 gilt-edged stock
4 default
5 maturity date
6 Treasury bonds
7 coupon
8 Treasury notes
9 yield
10 insolvent

33.2
1 true – The holders of bonds ... get their money ... back on a given maturity date
2 false – if a company ... declared bankrupt ... boldholders will probably get some of their money back
3 true – The highest grade (AAA or Aaa) means that there is almost no risk that the borrower will default
4 false – if interest rates rise, so that new borrowers have to pay a higher rate, existing bonds lose value
5 true – floating-rate notes ... whose interest rate varies with market interest rates
6 false – convertibles ... are bonds that the owner can later change into shares ... the buyer gets the chance of making a profit with the convertible option
7 true – zero coupon bonds ... pay no interest but are sold at a big discount on their par value
8 false – Bonds with a low credit rating (and a high chance of default) are called junk bonds

33.3 1 C, 2 C, 3 B, 4 B

34.1
1 spot price
2 backwardation
3 over-the-counter
4 forwards
5 commodities
6 to hedge
7 futures

34.2
1 A, x
2 B, z
3 B, v
4 A, w
5 B, u
6 C, y

34.3
1 true – currencies, interest rates, stocks and stock market indexes fluctuate ... so financial futures are used to fix a value for a specified future date
2 false – Interest rate futures are agreements to issue ... bonds, certificates of deposit, money market deposits, etc.
3 true – Interest rate futures are agreements between banks and investors and companies to issue fixed income securities ... at a future date
4 true – the buyer and seller of a financial future have different opinions about what will happen to exchange rates, interest rates and stock prices
5 false – Futures trading is a zero-sum game, because the amount of money gained by one party will be the same as the sum lost by the other

35.1 1c, 2a, 3b, 4d

35.2
1 a, d
2 b, c
3 b
4 a
5 a

35.3
1 Warrants
2 Put options
3 Swaps

35.4
1 premium
2 strike/exercise price
3 call options
4 warrants
5 swap

36.1 accumulate capital
allocate assets
allocate funds
allocate money
diversify portfolios
manage accounts
manage assets
manage money
manage portfolios

1 manage, assets/money/portfolio
2 diversify, portfolio
3 allocate, money/funds/assets
4 accumulate capital

36.2 1c, 2a, 3b

36.3 1c, 2d, 3a, 4b, 5e

37.1
1 to pool
2 to take a long position
3 to leverage
4 to take a short position

37.2
1 false – Despite their name, hedge funds do not necessarily use hedging techniques
2 true – Most hedge funds use gearing or leverage, which means borrowing money as well as using their own funds
3 false – they generally specialize in high-risk, short-term speculation
4 true – investors can profit from price differences between the two markets ... the price difference is usually very small (and would be zero if markets were perfectly efficient)
5 false – structured products from banks ... are customized ... financial instruments

37.3
1 Leverage
2 Capital Protection
3 Full Participation
4 Yield Enhancement

38.1 1c, 2a, 3b

38.2
1 remained stable
2 risen regularly
3 increased rapidly
4 grew slowly
5 sharp increases

38.3 Possible answer:
The price of gold rose steadily during 1985–7, reaching a peak of $500 an ounce at the end of 1987. The price fell again in 1988–9. The price fluctuated rapidly in 1990, and declined slowly during 1991–2. After a sharp rise in 1993, it remained stable for four years before falling dramatically between 1996 and 1999. Gold bottomed out at nearly $250 in both 1999 and 2001. Since 2001 there has been a steady rise to over $400.

39.1
1 acquisitions
2 joint venture
3 merger
4 raid, takeover bid

39.2
1 white knight, hostile
2 friendly
3 poison pill

39.3 1c, 2d, 3a, 4e, 5b

40.1
1 parent company
2 core business
3 asset-stripping
4 subsidiaries
5 leveraged
6 market capitalization
7 synergy

40.2 1b, 2d, 3a, 4e, 5c

40.3 1a, 2f, 3b, 4e, 5c, 6d

41.1
1 discounted cash flow
2 rate of return
3 internal rate of return
4 time value of money
5 purchasing power
6 discount rate

41.2
1 false – The return we could get by investing the money in other ways is the opportunity cost of capital
2 true – the rate of return must be at least as high as we could get by depositing the money in a bank instead, or by making another risk-free investment
3 false – there's nearly always inflation, so cash will have lower purchasing power in the future: you'll be able to buy less with the same amount of money
4 true – the value of money decreases over time

41.3 1b, 2e, 3d, 4c, 5a

42.1
1 price-sensitive
2 compliance
3 insider dealing
4 money laundering
5 fraudulent
6 disclosure
7 oversee

42.2 1c, 2a, 3e, 4b, 5d

42.3
1 laundering money
2 conflicts of interest
3 compliance officer
4 insider traders
5 Chinese walls
6 deregulation

43.1

					1 S										
2 B	3 A	L	A	N	C	E	O	F	T	R	4 A	D	E		
	B				A						D				
	5 S	U	R	P	L	U	S				V				
	O				E					6 T	A	R	I	7 F	F
	L										N			R	
8 Q	U	O	T	A					9 P		T			E	
	T							10 B	A	L	A	N	C	E	
11 D	E	F	I	C	I	T			Y		G			T	
U									M		E			R	
M		12 C				13 W			E					A	
14 P	R	O	T	E	C	T	I	O	N	I	S	M		D	
		S				O			T					E	
		T					15 V	I	S	I	B	L	E		

44.1
1 true – In theory, exchange rates should be at the level that gives purchasing power parity (PPP) … In fact, PPP does not work
2 false – if the price level in a country increases because of inflation, its currency should depreciate
3 true – Financial institutions, companies and rich individuals all buy currencies, looking for … short-term capital gains if a currency gains in value
4 false – currency speculation [is] buying currencies in the hope of making a profit … looking for high interest rates
5 true – currency traders make considerable profits from the spread between a currency's buying and selling prices
6 false – Over 95% of the world's currency transactions are purely speculative, and not related to trade
7 true – gold convertibility … ended in 1971, because … the Federal Reserve did not have enough gold to guarantee the American currency
8 true – For 25 years after World War II, the levels of most major currencies … were fixed … Since the early 1970s, there has been a system of floating exchange rates in most western countries
9 false – If there are more buyers of a currency than sellers, its price will rise; if there are more sellers, it will fall

44.2

Verb	Noun(s)	Noun for people	Adjective(s)
ap'preciate	appreci'ation	–	–
con'vert	converti'bility, con'version	–	con'verted
de'preciate	depreci'ation	–	–
inter'vene	inter'vention	–	inter'ventionary
'speculate	specu'lation	'speculator	'speculative

44.3
1 depreciate
2 appreciate
3 speculation
4 converting
5 speculators
6 intervene

45.1
1 true – a letter of credit … is a written promise by a bank to pay a certain amount to the seller … when the bank receives instructions from the buyer
2 true – a letter of credit … is a written promise … to pay a certain amount … within a fixed period
3 false – Documentary credits are usually irrevocable, meaning that they cannot be changed unless all the parties involved agree
4 false – the bill of lading is a document … confirming that the goods have been received for shipment
5 true – If a bill is endorsed by a well-known bank, the exporter can sell it … in the financial markets … This way the exporter gets most of the money immediately, and doesn't have to wait for the buyer to pay the bill
6 true – the exporter can sell it at a discount … When the bill matures, the buyer receives the full amount

45.2 1f, 2a, 3c, 4d, 5e, 6b

45.3 accept a bill of exchange
draw up a bill of exchange
endorse a bill of exchange
sell a bill of exchange
write a bill of exchange
prepare documents
present documents
require documents
sign documents
describe goods
receive goods
sell goods
transport goods

1 accepted/endorsed
2 describe
3 sell
4 signs, received
5 present

46.1
1 EXW
2 FCA
3 FAS
4 FOB
5 DES
6 DEQ
7, 8 CFR / CIF
9, 10, 11 DAF / CPT / CIP
12, 13 DDU / DDP

47.1

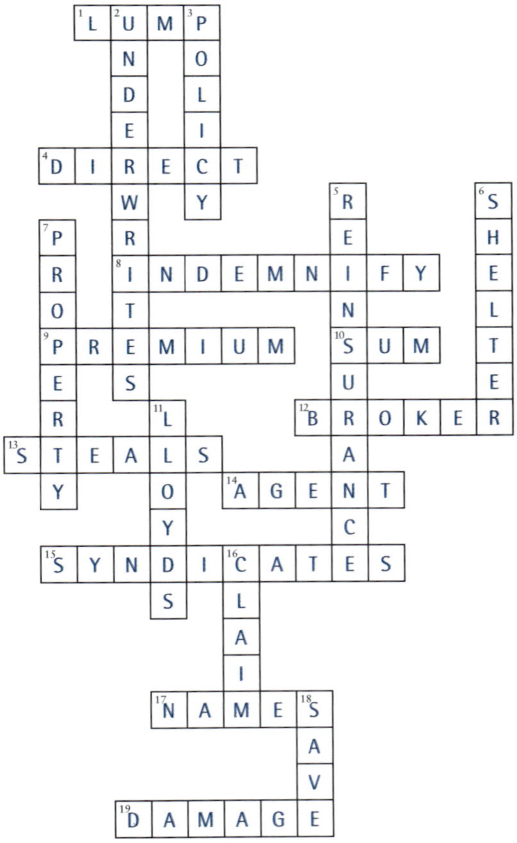

48.1

1 peak
2 downswing
3 recession
4 trough
5 recovery
6 boom

48.2 1d, 2e, 3c, 4b, 5a

48.3 to get bigger or make bigger: boost, expand, increase, inflate, raise, rise, reflate, stimulate
to get smaller or make smaller: contract, cool down, cut, decrease, deflate, reduce

49.1

1 excise taxes / excise duties
2 income tax / corporation tax
3 sales tax / value-added tax / goods and services tax
4 capital transfer tax / inheritance tax / estate tax / death duty
5 income tax and social security tax / national insurance
6 tariffs
7 capital gains tax

49.2

1 direct
2 proportional tax
3 social security
4 progressive tax
5 indirect

49.3

1 false – Most countries have a capital gains tax … at a much lower rate than income tax
2 true – Business profits are generally taxed twice, because after the company pays tax on its profits, the shareholders pay income tax on any dividends received from these profits
3 false – Indirect taxes such as sales tax and VAT are called proportional taxes, imposed at a fixed rate. But indirect taxes are actually regressive
4 true – excise duties [are] additional sales taxes on commodities like tobacco products, alcoholic drinks and petrol
5 true – Multinational companies often register their head offices in tax havens – small countries where income taxes for foreign companies are low
6 true – some employers give their staff … perks, such as company cars
7 false – Using legal methods to minimize your tax burden … is called tax avoidance
8 false – perks … loopholes [are] ways of getting around the law … called tax avoidance

49.4

charge tax
collect tax
impose tax
levy tax
pay tax

50.1

implement strategies
reach customers
require finance
supply services

1 supply, services
2 finance, require
3 implement, strategies
4 reach, customers

50.2

1 market opportunity
2 sales forecast
3 unique
4 marketing strategy
5 benefits
6 sales promotions

50.3

Finance: bear market, currency market, equity market, over-the-counter market, primary market, secondary market, stock market, market capitalization, market maker, market price, market value
Marketing: market penetration, market segment, market share, market skimming

Index

*The numbers in the index are **Unit** numbers not page numbers.*

Acknowledgements

I would like to thank Sally Searby at Cambridge University Press for commissioning this book. I owe a huge debt to my hawk-eyed and unremitting editors Joy Godwin and Lyn Strutt, who have had an enormous input into the book: the first draft was *very* different. I am grateful to Gareth Davies, Fiona Dunbar, Bridget Eakins and Rosemary Richey for their very useful comments on the first draft of the first half of the book. My thanks are also due to everyone involved in the design, production and marketing of the book.

Ian MacKenzie

The author and publishers are grateful to those authors, publishers and others who have given permission for the use of copyright material identified in the text. It has not always been possible to identify the source of material used or to contact the copyright holders and in such cases the publishers would welcome information from the copyright owners.

Barclays Bank PLC for adapted text on p. 18: 'Barclays Interim Report 2004', taken from the website www.investorrelations.barclays.co.uk. © Barclays Bank PLC. Used by permission; Pictet Asset Management UK Limited for text on p. 49: 'How can Pictet Help you?' taken from the website www.pictet.com. © Pictet Asset Management UK Limited. Used by permission; NatWest for text on p. 49: 'NatWest Personal Banking', taken from the website www.natwest.com. © National Westminster Bank Plc. Used by permission; UBS AG for text on p. 81, taken from the website www.ubs.com. © UBS 1998–2005. All rights reserved.

Photographs: p. 14 Corbis/Gabe Palmer, p. 15 Alamy/B.A.E. Inc, p. 50 Corbis/Jim Cummins, p. 52 Getty Images/RF, p. 62 Alamy/RF, p. 69 Alamy/Henry Westheim Photography, p. 74 Corbis/Reuters, p. 88 Alamy/RF, p. 90 Corbis/Simon Taplin, p. 93 Getty Images/Taxi, p. 94 Getty Images/AFP

Illustrations: Cartoon Bank pp. 22, 33; Cartoon Stock pp. 11, 24, 29, 44, 46, 54, 76, 80, 84, 86, 92, 101, 103; Kamae Design pp. 61, 69, 70, 99, 110